ADDISON-WESLEY OD SERIES

Managing Conflict

Second Edition

Interpersonal Dialogue and Third-Party Roles

Richard E. Walton

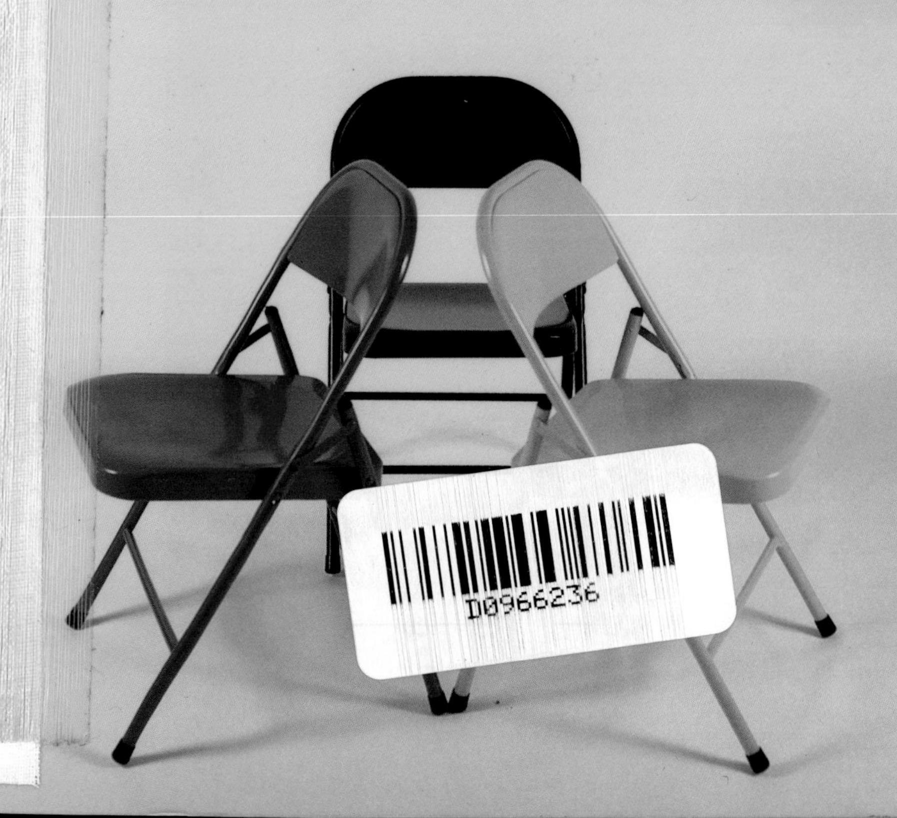

Managing Conflict

Second Edition

Managing Conflict

Interpersonal Dialogue and Third-Party Roles

Richard E. Walton
Graduate School of Business Administration
Harvard University

Addison-Wesley Publishing Company
Reading, Massachusetts • Menlo Park, California • Don Mills, Ontario • Wokingham, England • Amsterdam • Sydney • Singapore • Tokyo • Madrid • Bogotá • Santiago • San Juan

TO SHARON
partner in love and life

This book is in the Addison-Wesley Series on Organization Development.
Editors: Edgar H. Schein, Richard Beckhard

Other titles in the series:

Organizational Transitions:
Managing Complex Change, Second Edition
Richard Beckhard and Reubin Harris

Organization Development:
A Normative View
W. Warner Burke

Team Building:
Issues and Alternatives, Second Edition
William G. Dyer

The Technology Connection:
Strategy and Change in the Information Age
Marc S. Gerstein

Stream Analysis:
A Powerful Way to Diagnose and Manage Organizational Change
Jerry I. Porras

Process Consultation Volume II:
Lessons for Managers and Consultants
Edgar H. Schein

Library of Congress Cataloging-in-Publication Data

Walton, Richard E.
Managing conflict.

(The Addison-Wesley series on organization development)
1. Conflict management. I. Title. II. Series.
HD42.W35 1987 658.4 86–20679
ISBN 0–201–08859–2

ABCDEFGHIJ-BA-89876

Foreword

The Addison-Wesley Series on Organization Development originated in the late 1960s when a number of us recognized that the rapidly growing field of "OD" was not well understood or well defined. We also recognized that there was no one OD philosophy, and hence one could not at that time write a textbook on the theory and practice of OD, but one could make clear what various practitioners were doing under that label. So the original six books by Beckhard, Bennis, Blake and Mouton, Lawrence and Lorsch, Schein, and Walton launched what has since become a continuing enterprise. The essence of this enterprise was to let different authors speak for themselves instead of trying to summarize under one umbrella what was obviously a rapidly growing and highly diverse field.

By 1981 the series included nineteen titles, having added books by Beckhard and Harris, Cohen and Gadon, Davis, Dyer, Galbraith, Hackman and Oldham, Heenan and Perlmutter, Kotter, Lawler, Nadler, Roeber, Schein, and Steele. This proliferation reflected what had happened to the field of OD. It was growing by leaps and bounds, and it was expanding into all kinds of organizational areas and technologies of intervention. By this time many textbooks existed as well that tried to capture the core concepts of the field, but we felt that diversity and innovation were still the more salient aspects of OD today.

The present series is an attempt both to recapture some basics and to honor the growing diversity. So we have begun a series of revisions of some of the original books and have added a set of new authors or old authors with new content. Our hope is to capture the spirit of inquiry and innovation that has always been the hallmark of organization development and to launch with these books a new wave of insights into the forever tricky problem of how to change and improve organizations.

We are grateful that Addison-Wesley has chosen to continue the series and are also grateful to the many reviewers who have helped us and the authors in the preparation of the current series of books.

Cambridge, Massachusetts Edgar H. Schein
New York, New York Richard Beckhard

Preface

In recent years we have heightened our expectations for performance in organizations, typically out of competitive necessity. This applies not only to product quality and plant productivity, but to every managerial and professional activity in the enterprise. We expect greater excellence in activities as diverse as market planning, product development, systems implementation, and corporate communications.

Organizations can ill afford to dissipate the energy of their members in nonproductive conflict, and to distort organizational decisions by it. Still another force raises the stakes for the constructive management of conflict. In our search for greater effectiveness we are designing organizational forms that are flatter and delegate new functions to lower levels. They rely more on horizontal processes and less on hierarchical structures to resolve differences. And they rely more on shared goals and peer pressure and less on formal controls to achieve task coordination and compliance with organizational requirements. These and additional changes—broader jobs, more reliance on matrix and team structures, greater use of temporary task forces, and more numerous involvement mechanisms—all increase organizations' dependence on widespread diffusion of interpersonal skills, including the effective management of differences.

Thus, our organizational forms are fostering differences, are more vulnerable to poorly managed conflict, and are less tolerant of it. Fortunately, the requisite skills and attitudes have increased as well. Managers have become more conscious of the importance of understanding organizational and interpersonal processes and they have become personally more open to challenge by their colleagues about their views and behaviors.

Dialogue, the approach to conflict management described here, has become strategically valuable for organizations striving for higher standards of excellence and teamwork. It can be used today by more organization members, relying less on professionals, and in more informal and implicit ways than when it was proposed in the first edition over two decades ago.

Better dialogue has become more important between institutions as well as within organizations. Labor–management relations, for example, have been influenced by competitive pressures to move from adversarialism toward mutuality. In searching for the basis for a mutual relationship between institutions, their key representatives usually must transform the nature of their own relationships. Similar ingredients promote the success of dialogue whether the dialogue is between members of the same organization or representatives of labor and management. Each institutional setting presents its own unique requirements, but these generally are in addition to those set forth for the intraorganization dialogues, not in lieu of them.

I am indebted to the principals in the several conflict episodes reported here—in which I participated as the third-party consultant—for they subsequently assisted and encouraged me to document and derive the lessons from these practical ventures in conflict resolution. I also want to thank Ed Schein and Deborah Kolb for their helpful comments about this revision of the book.

Boston, Massachusetts R. E. W.

Contents

Managing Conflict

1

Introduction

This book proposes a theory and practice for managing conflict. I present a framework for diagnosing a recurrent conflict and suggest several basic options for controlling or resolving it. Most routes to better management of conflict involve a well-managed dialogue between the parties. I prescribe the functional ingredients which — if the dialogue is to be productive — must be ensured either by the parties themselves or by a third party. Then I analyze the many techniques that implement the necessary functions, such as those which set the time, place, agenda, and procedure for the dialogue. Finally, I propose the attributes needed by a third party who would provide the potential functions.

The dialogue concept and method are applicable to face-to-face work on conflicts that occur in a wide range of settings. The first three settings listed below are forms of intraorganizational conflict; the second three are forms of intersystem conflict.

1. Conflict between members of a family
2. Conflict confined to two individuals in an organization
3. Conflict between organizational units (manufacturing versus marketing, for example)
4. Conflict between institutions (as between union and management)

5. Conflict between ethnic groups or communities (racial conflict in the United States is one example)
6. Conflict between nations (Ethiopia versus Somalia, say)

As a third party I have facilitated the dialogue approach in each of these types of conflict settings, although they are not all illustrated in this book. The intraorganizational cases reported in Chapters 2 to 4 are either the second type, conflict confined to individual managers, or a combination of the second and third types, including interunit issues. The dialogue workshop in Chapter 9 is the sixth type, international. My current interest focuses on the fourth type, especially between labor and management. Interestingly, dealing with this intermediate setting draws directly upon techniques appropriate both to conflict illustrated in Chapters 2–4 and to the conflict in Chapter 9.

The general strategy of the book is to develop the dialogue approach using examples of intraorganizational conflict and then extend the approach to intersystem conflict. This chapter defines the terms of dialogue first in intraorganizational settings and then in intergroup settings.

Interpersonal Conflict in Organizations

Interpersonal conflict is defined broadly to include both (1) substantive disagreements such as differences over objectives, structures, policies, and practices, and (2) the more personal and emotional differences that arise between human beings.

The following are examples of conflicted relationships in organizational settings:[1]

1. Two managers needed to work together but continued to cancel each other's ideas and blunt each other's initiatives.
2. Members of a divisional staff were engaged in a disrup-

[1]These do not refer to the three cases analyzed in detail in Chapters 2–4.

tive conflict, which resulted in ill-defined goals and poorly coordinated activities.

3. Two members of a production team continually had disagreements that frustrated the development of the team's self-management capabilities.

In each case the conflict was continual, had become embedded in the relationships, and interfered with individual and joint performances.

Interpersonal relations in organizations are created by interdependencies involving physical work flows, technical services, information, or advice. One's actions may be controlled by the actions of another person just as one's performance may be evaluated by another. These and other interdependencies make conflict inevitable. Even if it were thought to be desirable, it would not be possible to create organizations free from interpersonal conflicts.

While conflict between organizational members is natural, indeed inevitable, direct approaches to dealing with this fact of organizational life are not. Several tendencies explain why.

Inhibitions are a factor. To express anger, resentment, or envy toward another member of a work organization may be considered bad manners or immature. But if these feelings are not expressed directly, they usually will be indirectly, often in ways that create still new conflict issues or incur other costs.

The immediate energy requirements also influence the way conflict is managed. It takes emotional energy to totally suppress the conflict, and it may take even more emotional energy to confront it. Therefore, conflicts often are played out in some indirect mode, which usually takes the least energy—in the short run. Indirect conflicts, however, have the longest life expectancy and have the most costs that cannot be attributed to the original conflict.

Another factor is risk. Important differences over policy and procedure may not surface because one or both of the principals fear that the conflict might create a residue of interpersonal antagonisms and hurt their careers. These risks are often real, but they can be minimized by understanding the ingredients for more effective dialogue and skill in supplying these ingredients.

The Dialogue Approach

The premise is not that interpersonal conflict in organizations is necessarily bad or destructive and that either those directly involved or third parties must inevitably try to eliminate or reduce conflict. Interpersonal differences, competition, rivalry, and other forms of conflict often have a positive value for the participants and the social system in which they occur. First, a moderate level of interpersonal conflict may increase motivation and energy. Second, conflict may promote innovation because it highlights diverse viewpoints. Third, the principals may develop increased understanding of their respective positions, because the conflict forces them to articulate their views and to bring forth all supporting arguments.

On the other hand, conflict can be debilitating for the participants, can rigidify the social system in which it occurs, and can lead to distortions of reality. Both the nature of the interdependence between the parties and the level of conflict will determine the nature of the consequences for the parties.

One can distinguish between resolution and control as different goals of conflict management. The principals themselves or a third party may attempt to gain resolution, so that the original differences or feelings of opposition no longer exist; or they may attempt to merely control conflict, so that the negative consequences of the conflict are decreased, even though the opposing preferences and antagonisms persist.

Conflict management may involve dialogue, but it need not. If the conflict between two managers is primarily a decisional conflict, about how to allocate resources between two projects, say, then it may be more appropriate for their supervisor to hear them out and make the allocation decision. If the underlying issue is already understood to result from contradictory role requirements, and if other interpersonal issues are already understood to be incidental to the conflict, then a structural change may be both appropriate to the task and helpful to the relationship. If there is a strong emotional component to the relationship and one or both of the parties can readily be transferred to another assignment, then terminating the relationship may be a good solution. Even if the conflict has a complex mix of substantive and emotional components and the relationship is one that would be costly to terminate, alternatives to dialogue must be considered. If by some means other than dialogue one or both of the principals gain the necessary insight into the dynamics of the conflict, then each may take unilateral steps to control the conflict, for example by avoiding the conditions that trigger conflict behavior.

Acknowledging these alternative solutions, let us turn to the dialogue option. *Dialogue* means that the parties directly engage each other and focus on the conflict between them, including aspects of their relationship itself.[2] Dialogue can be instrumental to either resolution or control. The constructive outcomes of the three conflict examples introduced are illustrative.

1. At the suggestion of their common superior, the two managers who persisted in canceling and blunting each other's contributions entered into dialogue about their differences. Each regarded the other as a rival for the same opportunities for promotion. With the assistance of an internal organizational consultant who had been working with the unit on other matters, the two managers identified what each person was doing to transform their normal rivalry into a destructive conflict. They resolved to learn how to manage both trust in their task relations and feelings of rivalry in their striving for advancement. They were largely successful.

2. The divisional managers whose conflict led to poor coordination and confusion about goals were brought into dialogue to explore their differences and find some basis for accommodation. Both personal style and contradictory role definitions were contributing to the ongoing conflict. The outcome: although they did not significantly change their respective personal styles of relating, they did modify and integrate their respective role definitions, and they moderated their emotional conflict.

3. The conflicting production workers were urged by other members of the production team to address their differences, in this case with the help of the team's supervisor, who wanted to accelerate the team's development of self-management capabilities.

---

[2]Subsequent discussion shows how direct attention to relationship issues differentiates the dialogue approach from stricter forms of negotiation and mediation.

The interpersonal conflict was traced back to an earlier incident in which each had misinterpreted the intentions of the other. Subsequent issues were symptoms and tactics resulting from the ensuing distrust. After a period of wariness, traces of this interpersonal conflict disappeared completely.

The basic objective of dialogue is to manage the conflict by resolution or better control, certainly to reduce its costs and, it is hoped, to improve the quality of the working relationship. A good working relationship has the following attributes.

- Identification of and commitment to the largest set of common goals appropriate to the co-workers' respective roles
- Mutually agreed roles
- Mutual trust and respect
- Shared norms and expectations
- Respect for individual differences and tolerance for diversity of views

Ideally the co-workers will be capable of effective and efficient communication and will find their relationship energizing rather than enervating. The importance of such attributes varies depending on task interdependence and context of the working relationship. However, they illustrate conditions that can result from better management of interpersonal conflict and can in turn enable better management of differences in the future.

When facilitated by a third party, the conflict management process described here can be educational or developmental for the participants, improving their skills for diagnosing conflict and resolving it through interpersonal dialogue.

The dialogue approach demonstrated in this book involved a third party, but the approach can work equally well for the conflict participants by themselves. It works well for two reasons. First, the diagnostic framework for analyzing the dynamics of interpersonal conflict offers to the participants themselves many of the same options for managing their conflicts it offers to would-be third parties. For example, it provides the participant the choice of entering into dialogue or taking other steps to control the conflict.

Second, the dialogue approach described here is based on a

functional theory; it prescribes the functional requirements that must be met for a dialogue to be constructive, acknowledging that an array of techniques can be utilized to meet them. The requirements include mutual reinforcement of motivation, balanced power in the situation, and an optimum level of tension. Thus, one or both of the parties themselves can attempt to assess the adequacy of these required ingredients. Preliminary assessment by a person considering a dialogue may establish that some of the specified conditions are already favorable and that the others can probably be implemented by the participants themselves. Many, but not all, of the possible mechanics by which these ingredients are provided can be implemented by the parties to the conflict.

Thus, with an understanding of the approach outlined in this book, one or both of the principals themselves can make more informed judgments, not only whether to enter into a dialogue, but also whether a third party is required, and if so, whether a colleague or a professional consultant is needed, and if not, what they themselves need to do to increase the effectiveness of their encounter.

We turn now to trends that underscore the need to consider the general relevance of the dialogue concepts and methods in organizational settings.

Trends in Organization and the Management of Differences

Several important trends have been underway in the last fifteen years, since the dialogue theory of conflict resolution was first proposed, affecting the way we should think about the problem and the approach to it outlined here.

One of the most fundamental environmental changes for the private sector in the United States has been increased competition from international firms or by new firms in deregulated industries. One direct effect of the heightened competition is that there is less tolerance for overtly individual-oriented or department-oriented behavior and more insistence that actions must be good for the organization as a whole. For this reason alone certain forms of intergroup behavior that were commonly observed a decade earlier appear to be somewhat less common in the 1980s.

Other indirect effects of heightened performance requirements on conflict and conflict management are even more significant. We are witnessing a profound transformation in the way organizations attempt to utilize human resources. The transformation includes the following features.

There is a trend toward flatter organization, with broader spans of control. Jobs or positions are more broadly defined, their requirements contingent upon changing task conditions. Team structures are used more, with the group rather than the individual defined as the accountable unit. There is more delegation of responsibilities for coordinating different functions to lower levels of the organization. And there is more use of project and matrix organizational forms, task forces, and participative problem-solving groups such as quality circles, as well as more forms of employee consultation.

These changes all affect conflicts to be managed because (1) they rely more on lateral coordination and less on hierarchical control, (2) they involve more *mutual* influence between persons at different hierarchical levels, (3) they deliberately design roles in which responsibility exceeds formal authority, (4) they expand the bases of influence beyond the more traditional concept of positional authority to include more dynamic factors like information and expertise, and (5) they involve inherently more ambiguity.

The net effect is to put a higher premium on interpersonal skills, including communication and conflict management. But that does not mean that the gap has increased between required and actual competencies. Fortunately, while the level of requirements for such competencies has been rising over the past decade, so too have the actual competencies. What is expected of managers and what is rewarded has changed. By the mid-1980s corporations in the United States had become much more sophisticated in managing change, in involving more stakeholders in decisions affecting them, and in designing and managing processes generally. For example, there was heightened appreciation that the quality of outcomes depends directly on the quality of the process.

The increased consciousness of process is especially important for the dialogue approach because, combined with the generally increased organizational skills, this greater attention to process has brought about a redefinition of the role of organization development as a specialization in the corporate organization.

The organizational development (OD) activity of the 1960s and early 1970s championed the idea that managers should develop their interpersonal competencies and skills in analyzing group process. Major corporations such as General Motors, IBM, and Exxon regularly sent participants to workshops that were designed to help managers become more effective in dealing with their peers, subordinates, and supervisors. These organizations also built internal consulting groups to help critique group processes, run team-building sessions, and the like. This was a period of consciousness raising about process.

What was then novel about process and skills is now often normal and institutionalized in these organizations. The social skills possessed by OD specialists in an earlier decade are now often possessed by the managers who would have been the clients a decade ago; the processes catalyzed and managed then by OD specialists are now more likely to be included as part of normal management.

Therefore today's edition of this book emphasizes even more than did the earlier edition the potential of team members, staff members, even organizational superiors to promote constructive dialogue between their colleagues who are experiencing persistent differences.

A further implication of these changes is that the types of assistance provided managers in conflict by colleagues often is more appropriately called "facilitation" than "third-party consultation."

There is a trend for resolution of conflict to occur in more varied and less formal ways than when it was exclusively the province of OD specialists. In recent years the types of dialogue described here have often occurred naturally and been facilitated relatively implicitly in organizational settings. The basic functional requirements have not changed; nor have the types of behaviors that provide those requirements changed in any systematic way. What has changed is the skill of the participants in dialogue, which has become greater, as has their reliance on organizational colleagues to provide the third-party facilitation required, especially if there has been an active OD group modeling processes and developing process skills.

Interpersonal Aspects of Intersystem Conflict

A second broad application of the dialogue approach is to the relationships between participants in intergroup conflict. Labor–management relations is an example. There has been an increased tendency in some industries for management to initiate basic change in union relations, often as a corollary of an effort to implement changes in work organization and methods, including greater employee participation. Management initiatives sometimes entail an off-site meeting with labor leaders to explore basic changes in their institutional roles and relationships. Effective dialogue in these meetings is often facilitated by third-party consultants. The basic dialogue concept and method have proven to apply. The same functional requirements (plus an additional one) must be met, similar intervention behaviors are tactical, and similar attributes are relevant to the third party's effectiveness.

The general relevance of the approach set forth here to intergroup settings is indicated by an analysis of an intergroup conflict resolution effort documented later in this book. The conflicts were border disputes in the Horn of Africa, where third-party intervention took the form of a problem-solving workshop whose participants were members of the governing elites of Somalia, Ethiopia, and Kenya.

Relation of Dialogue to Other Approaches to Conflict Management

The appropriateness of different approaches to conflict management depends importantly on the nature of the conflict. Three basically different processes are involved in the interaction between conflicting parties. The first process is *bargaining* over fixed-sum issues, in which what one party gains another must lose. The second process is *problem solving* to resolve variable-sum issues, in which, because the principals' underlying interests are not mutually exclusive, it is possible for them to identify these underlying interests and invent win/win solutions. The third process is *relationship structuring,* a process by which parties redefine or reinforce their mutual perceptions and attitudes, the meaning of their roles and relationship, and the norms that govern their interaction in the other processes.

These several processes are interrelated. Most of a party's actions directly instrumental to any one of these processes have side effects for one of the other processes. For example, openness in the service of problem solving may create vulnerability in the bargaining process. Also an irrevocable commitment instrumental to bargaining can hurt an established relationship.

The product of the third process, the state of the relationship, is a major factor determining how efficient and effective the parties will be in compromising their inherent differences via bargaining, and in intergrating their interests via problem solving. For example, the more mutual trust and respect, the more effective the substantively oriented processes, especially those involving a mixture of problem solving and bargaining.

How do the dialogue method and the third-party role relate to different combinations of these processes? Dialogue and, if necessary, third-party facilitation of the dialogue become appropriate when there is deemed to be a need to improve the quality of the future relationship or at least to improve the attitudes and understandings sufficiently to enable the parties to deal with acute issues or problems. However, when the salient processes are strictly bargaining or a combination of bargaining and problem solving, then mediation is the relevant third-party role.[3] In some circumstances, of course, this distinction between the mediator and the third-party role becomes a matter of emphasis. Mediation may need to generate a change in relations in order to obtain a resolution of the dispute in question; and the dialogue approach to improving a relationship may require the resolution of some substantive dispute at the heart of the deteriorated relationship.

[3]See Sheppard 1984; Kolb 1983; Bazerman and Lewicki 1985; and Hill 1982. Also see Pruitt and Rubin, 1986.

The basic premise underlying the emphasis on improving conflictful *relationships*, rather than resolving specific issues in conflicts, is that the quality of the relationship itself is a determinant of the performance of the parties to the relationship and their ability to handle future differences. Where this premise does not hold and the relationship is incidental, my emphasis is inappropriate and therefore the methodology taken as a whole is not relevant.

Comment on the Organizational Case Histories

Chapters 2 to 4 present three case histories involving two-party conflict and third-party assistance in organizational settings; they are then used illustratively in a broader analysis of the role of dialogue and third parties. While the cases later will be differentiated in many respects, two conditions common to them deserve preliminary comment.

First, in all three cases I was the third party. This means that the third party was an external consultant who was generally identified with an approach to organizational development involving openness and group process analysis. Second, the participants themselves had previously attended a human relations workshop that gave them practice in being open about their interpersonal reactions. These two conditions — the professional identity of the third party and the prior experiences of the two principals — enhanced the effectiveness of the third party's interventions documented here. When I first analyzed these cases this fact seemed more important to me than it does now. Since then I have had similar experiences working with parties who had never heard of a human relations workshop; and I have observed success in other situations in which third parties with very different professional identities were involved.

The Learning Strategy: Coupling the Roles of Practitioner and Researcher

Not only was I the actor in the third-party roles in the first three cases reported here, but the observer of the interaction of all three parties. This duality as practitioner and researcher-theorist has several implications.

During the episodes under consideration, many of the third-party interventions were either reflexive or intuitive. They took on purposeful definition only as I subsequently tried to first describe and then explain behaviors, including my own.

There are implications of the dual action-research role for the research product. Behavioral scientists usually insist that responsibility for the research and action aspects of a project inducing change be assigned to different persons. Thus, research and action would occur simultaneously in time and place but would involve two sets of behavioral scientists. This separation allows for objectivity in the research, and for singlemindedness of the action program. In contrast, the approach here was the opposite in the sense that the research and action involved the same behavioral scientist, but the two activities were in large part performed at different times and places. By coupling the third-party participant and observer roles, I eliminated the effect of the social-science observer, an effect that is always difficult to discount. Thus, typically, I had only to understand what was occurring in a system of three persons, all of whom were active and performing functions of immediate consequence in the interaction setting, rather than a system that included a fourth person in a strictly observer role.

I believe that the research strategy of coupling the third-party participant and observer roles, in contrast to separating them, has the following effects on the quality of observations and interpretation. On the one hand, the participant-observer has more complete knowledge of the intentions underlying the actions of the third party and the specific cues in the situation to which the third party is responding, as well as how the third party configured these cues into a diagnosis. On the other hand, participant-observers generally are somewhat less reliable in describing precisely their own manifest behavior and make less reliable inferences about the many possible effects of their own actions. They tend to be more selective in what is observed. Because of their responsibility in the situation, they will have hopes and fears that can result in either over- or underestimation of desired effects; moreover, they may be less attuned to unexpected results.

For objectives of the type of research reported here, I believe the advantages of coupling the participant and observer roles outweighed the disadvantages. Given that this research effort was intended to develop theory and give ideas operational meaning, rather than to test the merits of particular cause-and-effect relationships, it was somewhat more important to have a basis for inferring intention, reconstructing a diagnostic process, and identifying alternatives than it was to have strict objectivity in reporting effects and an accurate objective description of manifest behavior.

Notwithstanding this general conclusion, there was a brief but important period in one of the three cases reported here for which, as observer, I was not able to reconstruct the events, including my behavior. The period was the emotionally charged struggle between Mack and Sy at the staff meeting reported in Chapter 3. My faculties were attuned to the here-and-now, the process. I behaved intuitively and relied almost exclusively upon my own sixth sense. The support, reassurance, acceptance, and challenge that I felt I had provided each principal, the two of them as a pair, and the total group, were communicated in subtle nonverbal cues or in telegraphic comments that I was not able to isolate for description or analysis later. Thus, it must be acknowledged that, beyond some level of stress in the situation, if the stress is shared by the third party, the quality of the documentation of the process will deteriorate when the participant role and observer role are coupled.

The combination of practitioner and researcher improved my skills as the former, I believe. The discipline of reconstructing a relatively complete record of the behavior of the parties, and the discovery of patterns and meaning in the third party's actions, helped me evolve better diagnostic concepts and an appreciation for the importance of certain issues. For example, the degree of symmetry between two conflicting parties increasingly demanded my attention as a theoretical issue (a topic explored in Chapter 6) and, in turn, my actions as a third party became more attuned to this aspect of the dialogue situation. Thus, as a general proposition, the dual strategy of practitioner-researcher helps increase the likelihood that theories will be relevant to the world of action.

The fourth case, the Fermeda workshop on border disputes in Africa, occurred after the first edition of this book was written. It provided an opportunity to apply the ideas to a more complex conflict, in a more complex social setting. In this case I was one member of a third-party team. Other members of the third-party team have also written about the experience.

Although I was the third-party consultant in the three cases reported in Chapters 3, 4, and 5, I have elected to give the third party a fictitious name, Dave, just as I have given disguised names to other participants. This device helps distinguish between the thoughts and reasoning of the consultant in action and the researcher in analysis and reflection.

Plan of the Book

Chapters 2 through 4 present the three case histories of interpersonal conflict that provide most of the empirical material for the book. These will be developed generally in a way consistent with the methods used by the third party in gaining understanding of the conflict, its history, and its ramifications. The cases do not follow a common format. Each illustrates a somewhat different aspect of conflict dynamics and third-party function. Chapter 5 postulates a cyclical model of interpersonal conflict and argues its value as a diagnostic tool. Chapter 6 suggests that well-conceived dialogues can help in the resolution and control of interpersonal conflict and then postulates the strategic functions that promote constructive dialogue. Chapter 7 identifies the techniques and tactics used to manage the dialogue. The functions and the techniques can be performed by a third party; some of them by the participants themselves. Chapter 8 treats the problem of establishing and maintaining the appropriate third-party role. Chapter 9 extends the concept to intergroup conflict. Chapter 10 summarizes third-party functions, tactics, and desirable role attributes.

References

Bazerman, M. H., and R. J. Lewicki. "Contemporary Research Direction in the Study of Negotiations in Organizations: A Selective Overview." *Journal of Occupational Behavior* 6 (1985):1–16.

Hill, B. J. "An Analysis of Conflict Resolution Techniques: From Problem-Solving Workshops to Theory." *Journal of Conflict Resolution* 26 (1982):109–138.

Kolb, D. M. *The Mediators.* Cambridge, Mass.: MIT Press, 1983.

Pruitt, D. G., and J. Z. Rubin. *Social Conflict: Escalation, Stalemate, and Settlement.* New York: Random House, 1986.

Sheppard, B. H. "Third Party Conflict Intervention: A Procedural Framework." In L. L. Cummings and B. M. Staw, eds., *Research in Organizational Behavior,* vol. 6. Greenwich, Conn.: JAI Press, 1984.

2

Bill–Lloyd

Negotiating a Relationship[1]

In the case described in this chapter, the differences between two program directors in a government agency were negotiated with the help of a consultant. The third party's contribution appears to derive as much from attributes of the role in this case as from active intervention.

Background

Bill and Lloyd were program directors in the administrative services component of the agency. The third party, Dave, was a member of the external consulting staff of the agency's organizational development program. The program emphasized openness in interpersonal relations and utilized human relations training, workshops, and team-building experiences.

Bill was responsible for the development of a new system. He had been director of the Information Networks Program for

[1]This chapter is based on an article reprinted by permission of *J. Appl. Beh. Sci.*, 4, 3:327–50. "Interpersonal Confrontation and Basic Third Party Functions: A Case Study." © 1968 NTL Inst.

five months before the episode reported here, which occurred in January. It was uncertain that the system would ever be adopted, and he had to rely on several layers of supervision to represent his interests with the official who would decide. The uncertainty contributed to high turnover among better members of his staff. Moreover, he had to rely upon another group, the Systems Research Programs Staff (also within the administrative services component), to supply much of the professional talent required by the project. These factors affected morale within the professional staff and relations between Bill and George, the section head of the Systems Research Program who was responsible for that group's efforts on OSP.

Several months earlier the combined staffs working on OSP, including both Bill and George, had met in an off-site location to "build a team" and accomplish some program task work. Consultants on the organizational development staff, including the third-party consultant in this case, facilitated the team-building process. The meeting helped increase respect and trust among members of the total group and improve the integration of the two subgroups. Especially important for Bill was a better, if not perfect, understanding with George regarding their roles and personal styles. The whole group resolved not to allow the uncertainties of the OSP program to interfere with their work on the tasks at hand.

The operating style, which emerged from the off-site meeting and stabilized over the next several months, involved low structure (with roles loosely defined and changed according to the changing task demands) and more opportunity for professionals to influence their assignments. The fluid structure and the mutual-influence process required more time to be spent in group sessions. The meetings themselves were a mix of direct task work and group-maintenance work. Internal operations improved.

Lloyd became the Systems Research liaison to the OSP effort early in January when George was transferred. During the previous year, Lloyd, too, had been coping with problems of uncertainty about the future of the program of his group. He was acutely aware of the need to clarify and improve the group's status and functions in the agency. He had not become personally involved in the work on OSP. His subordinate, George, handled their personnel working on the project. However, Lloyd had heard from two members of this unit that the OSP project still did not have the direction and rigor they desired. When Lloyd assumed direct responsibility as liaison early in January, he wanted to review the entire OSP project, including the role of his staff and his own role.

One event in particular helped precipitate the conflict reported here. In a large meeting that included the combined staffs working on OSP, Lloyd made some statements that Bill found very disconcerting.

Later in January a casual meeting occurred involving Bill, his immediate superior, and Dave. The responsibility of Bill's superior included both Bill's and Lloyd's programs, as well as the organization development program. Bill mentioned his concern about Lloyd's participation in the combined staff meeting in particular and about their relationship in general. Bill was urged to confront Lloyd with his own concerns, to attempt to learn what prompted Lloyd to do what he did in the earlier meeting, and to try to establish a better working relationship. Bill decided to do this, and expressed a desire to utilize a consultant. Dave offered to participate.

The following day Bill first called Lloyd and set up a meeting in his office for later that morning and then called Dave asking whether he could attend. Dave agreed to attend, asking Bill to be responsible for explaining Dave's presence to Lloyd (who had never met Dave) and for getting Lloyd's concurrence for Dave to be present. Dave further said Bill and Lloyd were to determine how he could be helpful.

It appeared that Lloyd was dissatisfied with the role of his staff in OSP, with his role relationship to Bill, and with the operating style of the larger OSP project group, while Bill obviously had been satisfied with these factors. Lloyd's approach was to create an incentive for Bill to review these conditions. Bill acted quickly, partly in order to avail himself of Dave's presence as a third party on the scene. In any event, by the time they met in Bill's office, both had decided it was in their respective interests to discuss their relationship.

Starting the Meeting

Lloyd was present in Bill's office when Dave arrived. Bill introduced Dave as a consultant to the organization, whom he had asked to attend. He asked if Lloyd approved; Lloyd said he was glad to have Dave present. Dave asked Lloyd if he had attended one of the many training workshops that had been sponsored by the organizational development group. Lloyd indicated that he had; and Dave in turn identified himself as a member of the outside consulting organization that had been staffing the agency's workshops. This brief interchange tended to establish Dave's identity in a way appropriate for his third-party role.

Bill busied himself on other matters for several minutes, allowing Dave and Lloyd to become acquainted. During this time Lloyd did almost all the talking. Bill concluded his discussion and the three men moved to sit opposite one another in three comfortable chairs. The first topic was not pertinent to the relationship, and Dave excused himself for a few minutes. After Dave returned, they began to discuss their relationship.

The Opening Charges

Lloyd led off with a set of statements asserting differences between himself and George, with whom Bill had dealt previously. Also, Lloyd charged that there were "real gaps in the OSP design" that he was anxious to remedy when he became involved. His remarks also included the following points.

First, Lloyd charged that his own staff had not been allowed to contribute to the "strategic architectural, broad-design level" of the project; rather, they had been assigned the lower level "technical-computer work." Then Lloyd said, "What's more, if this is the type of resource talent you need, perhaps my staff should not be in the business of supplying this type of manpower."

Second, Lloyd observed that his staff had been defined as strictly advisory to Bill's group. He was uncertain that it was a viable arrangement for his staff to contribute resources without a role in decision making.

Third, he objected that under Bill's supervisory pattern professionals from the two groups were being assigned tasks in a manner that allowed him little or no leadership over his own professionals involved in the project.

He indicated that the status quo was unacceptable. He offered an alternative: to "break off" the members of his professional staff utilized by OSP and permanently reassign them to Bill's group, noting that would have the advantage of "freeing up (his program) to get new customers and do something else."

Lloyd's proposal sounded more like a bargaining tactic than a seriously proposed solution. Perhaps Lloyd was trying to exert pressure on Bill in order to create bargaining leverage and prove that he could not be taken for granted.

The Counterpoint

After failing repeatedly to break into Lloyd's long presentation of his views, Bill stopped trying to respond to Lloyd's points and challenged him directly for not allowing any response. Lloyd stopped abruptly, acknowledged the appropriateness of Bill's challenge, and resolved to listen.

Bill then recalled that he "had real trouble" with Lloyd's recent participation in the large meeting. He had not understood what Lloyd was trying to do. "In fact," he said, "I'm having some of the same reactions to what you have been saying here."

Bill's subsequent statements could be arranged as responses to Lloyd's assertions as follows:

First, Bill disagreed with the view that computer-technical contributions were of a "lower level" than the architectural, which he believed Lloyd's staff had been allowed to influence.

Second, Bill described his view of the client-consultant roles of the two groups: "Systems Research staff should make resources and advice available to the Information Networks staff who then have final decisions on design and the responsibility for working with the line organization." Thus, he acknowledged their differences on this point.

Third, Bill defined his working style, claiming that it had not detracted from the leadership role of Lloyd's predecessor, George. Bill assured Lloyd that he would respond to any concerns of this kind when they arose.

After both had had an opportunity to express themselves and make rebuttals Bill asked Dave for his observations. Before

Dave could respond, Lloyd said he wanted to ask Bill directly whether he would want several members of Lloyd's staff if their positions could be transferred. Bill objected that such a transfer would never be approved and, therefore, he saw no reason to give it further thought. Besides, his need for the talent in question was temporary, which argued against any transfer.

Digging Deeper: From the Intergroup to the Interpersonal Level

When Dave did speak, he suggested that the interchange could be characterized as a negotiation, with Lloyd in effect saying, "Here are my requests, which must be given due consideration if my staff is going to continue to contribute to OSP." Dave sharpened the issues that Lloyd had put on the agenda, citing both Lloyd's view and Bill's answer, in much the same terms as reported above. After discussing these points, they identified other concerns.

Lloyd was uncomfortable with the operating style under Bill's leadership: it was too loose, unstructured, and "groupy." He preferred more "crispness" and structure. In contrast, Bill was pleased with the group operation and did not want Lloyd to try to change it. Lloyd indicated with increasing emphasis that Bill was going to have to consider his preferences.

Lloyd also said that he had some general ideas on the OSP, but he had not yet been given enough information about the project to test his ideas. Therefore, he wanted an early review of the project. Later in the discussion, he acknowledged that one of his underlying concerns was in "getting connected" with the project and also in being recognized as an experienced and competent person on the project team. He underscored this desire to be seen as competent to Dave in a conversation while Bill was handling one of several telephone calls that interrupted the meeting. Lloyd enumerated past experiences in which he had had full responsibility for developing such systems.

For his part Bill failed to indicate an interest in what Lloyd could contribute, nor did he seem to acknowledge Lloyd's apparent desire to be recognized in this respect. To Dave, it appeared that Bill's inattention to Lloyd's needs might be related to the latter's attacks on the performance of Bill's group, and vice versa.

Dave observed to them that these subtler interpersonal issues could serve to keep them apart.

The outcome of the session was to schedule a meeting of both groups to review the work and further improve the work processes. As the session concluded, Bill expressed satisfaction that there was more mutual understanding. Dave asked to meet with each person to discuss the meeting and to determine whether he could be of any further help. Both agreed that this was desirable.

The principals had styles and skills that increased the likelihood of a successful dialogue. Lloyd's directness was one asset, ensuring the issues would be recognized. Bill's understanding of interpersonal processes enabled him to hear Lloyd out and also to challenge his domineering manner.

The third party listened to each of the disputants discuss his views and sharpened what he understood to be an issue, which the participants could confirm or challenge. These issues were stated in ways that made each person's position understandable, legitimate, and acceptable. One apparent effect of this understanding, legitimating, and sharpening of issues was to encourage Lloyd then to identify the more personal concerns he had about not being recognized and utilized.

The third party chose to play what he regarded as a minor role in regulating the process. Essentially, he let the parties run on their own. For example, he waited for Bill to deal first with the way Lloyd was dominating the discussion. Thus, he believed that the two parties had an opportunity to reveal or develop their own interaction equilibrium. Nevertheless, Lloyd attributed an active role to Dave. After reading this report he said:

> I believe the report understates Dave's effect as a third party and casts him more outside the process than I experienced him. Both his presence and his active, constructive participation influenced the process. For example, he turned me off once when I was getting long-winded, reminding me of the need to listen. When you hear something from a third party who doesn't have an investment in the issues at stake, you are more likely to respond to that advice, especially if it is given to you in a timely way on the spot. . . . In sum, for me, he was not only a catalytic agent, but also an ingredient in the situation.

Postconfrontation Reactions and Developments

Late that afternoon, Bill told Dave in convincing terms that the session with Lloyd had been productive. He believed that he and Lloyd understood each other better and could continue the dialogue. In his opinion, the presence of the consultant had encouraged a genuine confrontation.

Several days later, after the review meeting between the two groups had occurred, Lloyd reported that although differences remained between Bill and himself, they now could manage these differences.

Lloyd's remarks indicated reduced concerns about whether the resources of his staff were being used productively and the operating style of the combined groups. He continued to be critical of the "cold, hard fact that Bill doesn't have anyone on his staff who has been through this." He now had another reason not to press for an immediate resolution of issues about the roles of the two groups. In talking with his superior he gained a better appreciation of the provisional nature of the structure of the development effort. He seemed satisfied that if and when there was a decision to go ahead on the project, the present structure would not prejudice the form that the eventual one would take.

Lloyd commented:

> We have made headway. . . . I am more relaxed about the way things are going. . . . I came away from the meeting with a better understanding of Bill's position . . . and I know Bill better understands my position. At the larger group meeting Bill summarized our discussion in his office and I was satisfied with it. . . . We have openness going for us.

Lloyd said that Dave had been helpful and that it would be desirable to keep a consultant involved "who was familiar with the developing situation, but who could take a spectator position."

Several months later, Bill read this report and added:

> Against a longer time frame, the results were even better than the report conveys. Lloyd is accustomed to more

> structure than we had in the total group. Nevertheless, within a month, we were operating very well, and he felt as much at home as anyone. Through understanding the personal needs he communicated during that session in January, we found that his participation in the project became both visible and valued.

Dave also learned that Lloyd had developed high regard for Bill over the same period.

Conclusion

What were the potential and actual outcomes of the confrontation between Bill and Lloyd? Against the background of possible mounting tension, it reversed the cycle and achieved a trend of de-escalation. The immediate effect was to help the parties clarify the intergroup issues. For examples, Lloyd cited Bill's ability to state Lloyd's position as evidence that Bill understood. They made even more rapid progress in eliminating the interpersonal conflict: within a couple of weeks Lloyd reported feeling more relaxed, and noted that he and Bill "have openness going for us." Later Bill reported that within a month Lloyd "felt as much at home as anyone" with Bill's operating style and that Lloyd's participation had become "both visible and valued." Their improved rapport enabled them to handle the remaining intergroup issues more effectively.

The influence of the third party resulted in part from active contributions (regulating interaction, sharpening issues, and diagnosing the relationship). More surprising were the basic functions performed in a passive way — by his mere presence. His encouragement of the confrontation in the first place derived from the participants' expectations about him (support, process skill, learning, and insight) and from the symbolic meaning attributed to him as a result of his identification with a class of persons (workshop leaders) with whom the participants had had an intensive and successful experience. In the following two cases, active interventions into the ongoing process and individual work with the participants were more important aspects of the third-party role.

3

Mack–Sy

Confronting a Deeply Felt Conflict

The conflict reported here occurred between two managers of a division of a large manufacturing firm. As in the preceding case, the conflict has both interpersonal and interdepartmental aspects. However, the interpersonal and, in particular, the emotional dimensions are relatively more salient in the conflict analyzed in this chapter. The third-party consultant played an active role in the phases of the conflict episode that took place during two visits to the organization over a period of four months. The chapter provides a background description of the organization and an account of the conflict.

Background

The immediate organizational context for the conflict between Sy (the assistant director) and Mack (the controller) was the management staff for the Indianapolis division operations. Corporation headquarters were located in Detroit. Lines of both industrial and consumer products were processed and manufactured at Indianapolis.

Turnover in these staff positions was high. None of the present staff had been in the same position over a year. Most of their predecessors had been promoted. Two had left the company. All members of the present staff aspired to higher positions, but they were aware of the "up or out" character of Indianapolis assignments. To be promoted, a manager on the Indianapolis staff usually had to have *both* a sponsor in Detroit and the positive evaluation of the director.

The third-party consultant, Dave, had worked with the division for fifteen months. During one-day visits he observed staff meetings and led critiques of the group process. He also met with staff members individually, discussing organizational problems or concerns, and sharing his own perceptions of their effectiveness in the staff meetings.

The staff meetings were usually low-key, marked by some humor. More time was spent exchanging information than making decisions. There was little open disagreement, although a stated norm favored openness. They occasionally tried to review, analyze, and improve the process of their own staff meeting when the consultant was not present by saying, "Let's do what we would if Dave were here."

The present director had strong and open relationships with most members of his staff. He initiated periodic discussions with subordinates about their working relationship, giving and asking for candid reactions and evaluations. However, this type of openness had not developed among members of his staff.

The director had a strong "management development" agenda for the use of the consultant. In addition to trying to establish a productive relationship, he wanted the feedback for himself and others, to make each of them more effective managers. Instrumental in promoting the openness and the desire to develop more interpersonal competence were workshops attended by the director and many members of his staff.

The consultant, who was on sabbatical leave on the West Coast, had not visited Indianapolis for six months. After he agreed to spend two days at the division during a planned trip to the Midwest, he received a call from the director. The performance of the division was below expectations, due in part to operations at Indianapolis. In addition, a power struggle had developed among the director's superiors.

The director commented on each member of his staff. He indicated high satisfaction with development of Sy, his assistant director, who was serving as his primary soundingboard. Regarding Mack, the controller, he said:

> Mack is a young fellow who doesn't want to be a controller. He is aggressive and competent. He is so damned aggressive that he often drives people out of a discussion. That even happens to me. I'll leave a discussion with him all frustrated. But he just got back from a sensitivity training lab and he said he got feedback from his group about his aggressiveness. We just had a wonderful lunch together and he reported his lab experience. He also reported that during a very difficult episode in the group he had waited and then come quietly into the discussion and to his surprise they had listened to him and took his ideas. I was pleased that he had that lesson. However, in a recent meeting, he reverted back to type, and became aggressive.

The director also reported an episode in the last staff meeting.

> Yesterday Sy and Mack were in coflict. Sy brought it into the open. He had put on the agenda "controller responsibility." This was the first I knew about it. Mack contended his job was to give figures upward, not downward. Sy couldn't buy this. One of Sy's subordinates had raised the issue in the first place. In the meeting, this subordinate said that the controller area was a service area and that his employees weren't getting service. Well, I broke in and tried to set this fellow straight; I said, "When you vie for service, you still have to get it through persuasion."

This comment was the director's only reference to the conflict between Sy and Mack and was made in passing.

On the first of a two-day visit, the consultant scheduled discussions with as many members of the staff as possible. During interviews with Mack and Sy, Dave only vaguely recalled the director's fleeting reference to the incident at the staff meeting. He had no plans to focus on this interpersonal relationship.

Discussion with Mack

The consultant's session with Mack centered mostly on his recent workshop experience. It was easy to listen empathically to Mack. He was concerned about his current job and his work relationships. His current assignment as controller required analytical behavior, whereas he preferred to be "intuitive." Although this was a promotion, he questioned whether he should have been taken out of production. He was disappointed that an acquisition project (the X Mill project) for which he had been responsible was given to Sy to operate. He implied that he had withheld some energy from his work, reporting, for example, that he put in less time outside regular office hours than formerly.

Mack was perplexed about how much of the openness and spontaneity he had learned in the workshop could be used in the organizational situation. He felt an "intense conflict" with another person in the staff group, whom he "knew" he "had to confront"; to date, he had not been ready to follow through. He asked for advice on how to apply the workshop learning. The consultant suggested that there was an optimum time lag after an intense workshop experience before undertaking work on tough interpersonal issues. Mack did not offer to identify the person with whom he was in conflict and the matter was dropped. Later, it became apparent that he was referring to his relationship with Sy.

Discussion with Sy

Sy identified several working relationships he wanted to improve, including those with his subordinates and with the new personnel manager. He was "especially concerned" about a poor relationship with Mack.

Sy saw Mack as disinterested in the division's success and preoccupied with his own career. Although Sy did not cite particulars, two possibilities presented themselves. First, the director (but not Sy) mentioned a recent incident in which Mack had accommodated the corporate controller in Detroit who asked him to delay providing performance data to the division staff and the director's line superior. Second, Sy was annoyed that when he assumed responsibility for the X Mill project, Mack essentially "washed his hands" of the matter, withholding any assistance. Sy deeply resented Mack's attempts to dominate their discussions. Sy cited a recent discussion in which he was trying to get as much assistance as possible from Mack. Paradoxically he, Sy, ended the discussion because of Mack's manner, even though he was dependent upon Mack for information and advice.

After Sy seemed to have exhausted his thoughts about Mack, Dave said:

> You know, I'm sitting here considering the difference in our reactions to Mack. Earlier today I had a session with Mack in which I reacted very positively and felt quite friendly toward him. It's true it was just one session, and a special type at that, but I wonder what unique aspects of your relationship with Mack account for your feelings toward him.

Shortly afterwards, Dave added, "I wonder what *you* bring to that relationship." He also pondered another question: "Given your long list of negative feelings about Mack, is one of these basic and are the others just reflections of this central concern? Do you have any hunches?"

Sy explored this question. He seemed to center on the issue of trust. He related an instance where he had not consulted Mack in making a promotion decision about one of Mack's former subordinates, although it would have been appropriate for him to do so. "I guess I didn't trust him to keep it to himself." Sy concluded that he was going to have to confront his differences with Mack.

Dave began to consider the idea of working with the two men as a pair during his visit. The original schedule had committed all of Dave's time. However, it was 4:45 P.M. and perhaps plans could be changed to accommodate a get-together over drinks after work. Without yet deciding to try to arrange for a dialogue, he shared the idea with Sy. Sy responded favorably and was prepared to shift some important family commitments. Dave was ambivalent. He walked over to Mack's office and confirmed that Mack was still there. Dave asked himself, "Is Mack ready? Are Sy and Mack going to confront anyway? Do I want to be responsible? How much energy do I have available after a strenuous day and several days before that?"

Dave decided to meet if Mack was available and told Sy, who immediately went to Mack's office to invite him to meet for drinks. It occurred to Dave that it might have been better for him (rather than Sy) to have invited Mack. Sy returned to indicate that they had agreed to meet at 5:30 P.M. at the club.

Dave informed Sy that the personnel manager, who expected to meet Dave after work, would probably join them at the club. Dave contacted the personnel manager about the change in plans and explained briefly that he hoped Sy and Mack could work on what appeared to Dave to be important interpersonal issues. The personnel manager offered to stay away, but Dave said he might be helpful and in any event his involvement would assist in building an internal consulting role.

Meeting After Work: Trying to Get the Issues Joined

After all four persons had arrived and engaged in some chitchat, Dave said, "My thinking about this meeting included the possibility that we do some work on relationships."

After a pause, Sy turned to Mack: "I feel antagonistic toward you, and find it very difficult to work with you. I want to understand why and do something about it if possible."

Mack reacted quickly. His response took the form of emphasizing that he and Sy had very different styles of working: he is intuitive, Sy is methodical; he tries to make money for the company by spending money, Sy by saving money; he had a broad view, Sy was a detail man. His discussion then turned to center on himself: the bad fit between his style and his controller's job, and his recent disappointment in losing the X Mill project, and more.

Mack went on at some length. Although it is not fully apparent from the summary of Mack's response, at the time it appeared to Sy, Dave, and the personnel manager that Mack was no longer responding directly to Sy. The personnel manager finally interrupted Mack.

The personnel manager (in a scolding tone): You are not responding to Sy and his feelings.

Mack: What do you mean?

Dave: You seemed to be describing a set of factors affecting you. Can you link that up to your relationship with Sy?

Mack's response indicated reluctance to confront Sy, and he suggested that it was up to Sy to proceed if he liked. Sy then repeated a theme that had occurred in his earlier discussion with Dave.

Sy: I don't know why you bug me; it is more than that we are different. . . . Is it that I don't like you trying to dominate me, or could it be that I don't trust you?

(Mack did not respond.)

Dave (to Sy, who seemed to be disappointed that Mack hadn't responded): Actually there is not much Mack can do with the question phrased that way. Can you supply more of the perceptions and other background upon which your feelings are based?

In reply to Dave's request for him to cite instances that had influenced his attitude toward Mack, Sy recalled that he had not consulted Mack regarding the promotion of a former subordinate of Mack's, "apparently because of a lack of trust." Mack, in turn, confirmed that he did indeed resent not being informed and that he had not understood why he was not contacted.

Later, Sy identified another issue. "We need more controller work, more data for us in production." Mack responded, "You, Sy, do more controller's work than I do. You go over reports so thoroughly that I count on you to catch errors. Also, it's up to you to decide what your problems are. I've done all a controller can do."

Both this interchange and the preceding one seemed only to scratch the surface of the issues and feelings involved. Sy tried still another issue.

Sy: One thing I can't accept is your response to the X Mill project. I *need* you to help me with that project. You've got the background information and the abilities which are needed. But when you didn't get overall responsibility for the project, you withdrew completely. I just can't accept your saying, "If I'm not *the* man, I won't contribute."

Mack: But that's how I am. That's how I feel.

(Sy's shoulders slumped and he turned the palms of his hands upward in a gesture of futility.)

Dave (both to give Sy some support and to confront Mack): It's hard to deal with that position.

At a later point, as if to suggest that one of the reasons he could not contribute to the X Mill project had to do with his feelings toward Sy in particular, Mack said, "I must say that I'm concerned about working *for* you when that happens." (Mack was referring to the likelihood that Sy would be the next division director within a year or so.)

Mack was paged for a telephone call, and while he was out of the room, the other three sat silent for a moment. Dave asked Sy, "How do you feel? Do you feel that you and Mack have engaged each other this evening, or have been semiengaged, or not at all?" Sy responded, "Semiengaged."

When Mack returned, Dave reported his question to Sy and Sy's answer, and asked Mack how he felt. He, too, felt "semiengaged" with Sy.

Both said that this had represented the start of a necessary dialogue and wanted to keep working on the issue when there was an opportunity. Dave later realized that it might well have been advisable to encourage them to agree upon a specific time to meet and resume their dialogue.

The meeting was ended because Sy, Dave, and the personnel manager all had to leave for other engagements. During the phone call, Mack had had his evening appointment canceled so that he was free the rest of the evening. Dave explained why he had to leave, and also that Sy had indicated to him earlier that he had to leave. (Dave was concerned that Mack not feel rejected.)

Dave was driven to his motel by Mack, who said that he felt the confrontation was cut short. He had much stronger feelings about Sy that had not come out yet, and he had very deep concerns about what would happen if Sy became the director and, thus, his boss. On the other hand, in response to a direct question, he said that he did not feel that he was taking great personal risks in the dialogue. There was no time to pursue this last, puzzling remark then.

Staff Meeting: Sy's Outburst

Thursday morning was the regularly scheduled weekly staff meeting. The director and six members of his staff were present; only one member, the consumer products manager, was absent. It was a typical meeting up to the point late in the meeting when an incident occurred between Sy and Mack. However, certain events or processes appeared to be related to the Sy–Mack relationship. First, Mack shared with the staff the contents of a controller's "confidential" report, noting that his disclosures to the staff were contrary to the preferences of higher controller officials in Detroit. Dave thought this act may have been a conciliatory overture to Sy and the group.

The second event was an instance in which Mack was quite aggressive. The topic being discussed was the need for a general manager for the industrial products operations, which were showing up poorly in the performance record. The sales and manufacturing managers of industrial products had both reported to the director until recently, when an organizational change resulted in their reporting to Sy, as the assistant director. A general assumption had been that a separate general-manager position ought to be created; however, neither the present sales manager nor the manufacturing manager was deemed qualified to handle the job of general manager. Mack pressed the director, challenged his assumptions, and told him what he ought to do. The director exercised restraint and used Mack's ideas without fighting back. However, Mack's aggressiveness in this interchange with the director may have triggered something within Sy that later contributed to his outburst at Mack.

At the conclusion of the business meeting, Dave led a critique of the group's processes. Dave compared the meeting with earlier staff meetings he had observed when the group had a somewhat different composition. The meeting had been relatively uneventful, and Dave's observations sharpened only a few procedural issues or interpersonal interchanges, including the one between Mack and the division director. Mack again made a powerful, repetitive, insistent, but somewhat general, assertion to the director that the need for a new reporting relationship was great because the industrial operations were doing so badly.

Mack was still going strong when Sy interrupted him with an almost violent outburst, pounding the table, turning toward Mack and slamming his fist down on the table in front of Mack. Sy was very, very angry.

Sy: Damn it, you keep saying that [that the industrial operations are going badly], but when I try to get you to work on it you don't!

Mack: Wait a minute, the last time I tried in the meeting a week ago — it was *you* that didn't want to continue!

Sy (countering): I broke off the meeting when I couldn't absorb any more.

Sy and Mack argued the point further for a few minutes. Then Mack shifted the focus and repeated twice his personal feelings about the controller's work and his suitability for that job. Then, Mack was confronted with the fact that he had again turned attention to his job when his relationship with Sy was being discussed.

Dave: I have come to a new hunch about your behavior. Are you trying to *prove* that you are *not* suited for the controller's job? . . . There are two hypotheses. First, that you are trying to minimize the effects of the mismatch between your style and the controller job. Second, that you are trying to illustrate, dramatize, demonstrate, and prove the mismatch.

Mack: I am trying to minimize the effects of the mismatch, but it's true that I have started to evaluate whether this company is the place for me. (He went on to say that it might be wise for him to consider another firm.)

Sy: I believe it's the second of Dave's hypotheses: that you are trying to convince others of the mismatch. (Sy elaborated on this perception.)

Dave (to Mack): It's possible that at some level you really are trying to make this point, whatever the consequences.

Then at another point, Dave attempted to assess the mutuality of their feelings of dependence on each other:

Dave (to Mack): Do you feel dependent on Sy? He has said he feels dependent on you, but I haven't heard you say anything like that.

Mack: No, I don't.

Dave: To the extent that you have defined the situation in that way, it's very difficult to work on this thing.

The words recorded here do not convey the emotionally charged confrontations between the two principals in this case. The others at the staff meeting also appeared deeply concerned, though none of them ventured into the conflict during this session.

At the end of the staff meeting the consultant made the following remarks to the pair and to the others present.

> I'm not sure there is a solution. Mack, the fact that you don't feel dependent on Sy makes it more difficult. You are both strong and you are both open about your negative feelings — these are the encouraging factors. One of the problems is that your personal styles may clash so much that you generate new interpersonal issues, even while you're talking and trying to work out existing differences. That's where others can help.
>
> Sy and Mack have different things to offer this staff. It would be a shame for the organization to lose Mack. Mack has certain unique strengths to offer. It's a challenge to find a way to make it possible for Mack to work on Sy's task problems. In part, it's up to you, Mack, to say how others can help make it possible for you to work productively. It is important for the two of you to keep talking.

In concluding the staff meeting, he suggested that they all go to lunch; the director suggested they go to "the club." On the way out of the office building, the personnel manager said to Dave, "I was moved; that's all I can say." All six rode to the club together.

Before the staff meeting, no one but Sy was aware of the depth of his aversion to Mack. The director had only mentioned the earlier debate between Sy and Mack. The personnel manager had not made any mention of this conflict in sharing with Dave his perceptions of the current personal and organizational issues. Prior to the staff meeting, when Sy had said, "I wonder why I feel the way I do toward Mack," he appeared to be puzzled or perplexed, but not highly disturbed.

Sy's tension had mounted after the evening meeting, apparently out of frustration in failing to engage Mack. This frustration, plus Mack's further provocative behavior during the staff meeting, must have led to Sy's outburst, which in turn pushed the overall tension to a very high point. This intense confrontation was a climax of the mutual antagonism and undoubtedly set the background not only for the quiet, reflective work that afternoon but also for the improvements that were to come much later.

Rest, Recuperation, and Repair

After they had arrived, ordered drinks, and handled some miscellaneous business items, the director asked Dave what the group should talk about.

Dave deliberately tried to avoid further work on the Sy–Mack relationship during that lunch. Therefore, he raised a question about the pattern of his future work with the staff, suggesting two or three alternative patterns. As a part of the discussion that followed, they explored a misunderstanding. Apparently, the personnel manager had misinterpreted the staff's interest in getting Dave to come several weeks earlier. One person questioned the personnel manager, asking whether he agreed with having Dave work with the staff. The personnel manager said he definitely did agree. Dave himself expressed some irritation with the personnel manager's handling of the visit and chided him for being a "hard-nosed negotiator." (In this interpersonal interchange, Dave was a principal. That fact may have facilitated what followed.)

Mack commented that he believed last night had been "rigged." At first, Dave was taken aback by the comment. Addressing himself to Mack, Dave reconstructed his own thinking and his discussions with Sy and the personnel manager that had led to the evening meeting. Dave confirmed that the dialogue had been planned for, but he did not accept that it had been rigged. Nevertheless, Mack added, "I'll never trust you again."

As the group moved from the cocktail lounge to the luncheon table, Dave commented in a half-humorous way to the group, including Mack, "I thought it was clear that I had a white hat. Now I learn that Mack saw me as wearing a black hat."

Mack then reflected ambivalence about the episode by saying, "This type of candid reaction to me and my style of operating is precisely what I wanted from my sensitivity-training group, but didn't get."

There were long lapses in the conversation during the cocktail session and the protracted lunch that lasted to midafternoon. People were reflecting upon the morning confrontation and its meaning for them, and generally resting by engaging in light conversation. The additional discussion directly relevant to the Sy–Mack episode dealt with Mack's ambivalence about the confrontation and his feelings about Dave's role in it.

Dave (to Mack): I'm concerned about the trust issue. That hits me in the most crucial aspect of my role with this group. I'd like to hear more about what you're thinking or feeling.

Mack: It's not really trust. I just don't know. I've taken some big risks. My own career's on the line. At least my future with this company.

Dave: What is the risk? How is it likely to affect your future with the company?

Mack: Sy will remember this. He can't help but take it into account. It's bound to work against me.

Dave: I see what you mean. . . . Only the future will tell. There just is no way for us to know now. Asking Sy still wouldn't give you an answer to this . . . but for what it's worth, my sense of Sy's integrity, his discipline, his notions of fairness, these all tell me that he won't use this interchange or what you revealed about yourself against you. . . . In fact, as I reflect on it, maybe you are projecting some of your own inclinations onto Sy. In a way, compared with you, Sy is less likely to be worrying about his career and thinking politically.

Dave (to Mack after a lapse): As for how you perceive my role in this confrontation, let me add still more detail about what preceded the decision to try and get some dialogue going between you and Sy. When I was talking with Sy yesterday afternoon and he was describing his negative reactions to you, I admitted to him that I didn't have the same reaction to you. I had felt quite positive toward you on the basis of our interview; therefore, I said to Sy, I wonder how much of that is Mack and how much is you, Sy.

Notwithstanding his anxiety about the risks he had taken in the confrontation, Mack signaled in several ways that he wanted Dave to continue to work with the staff, with himself, and perhaps also with his subordinates.

Dave's suggestion that they go to lunch together held the group intact following their high emotional experience; this allowed members to provide each other with the reassurance they needed. Also, each member of the group was given an opportunity to reflect on the experience and find some meaning for himself. Fortunately, the director and other members of the staff manifested a mature acceptance of the morning's confrontation. This undoubtedly went far in reducing the fears of disapproval that the participants might otherwise have entertained.

Touching Bases Before Departure

When the group returned to the office, Dave dropped in on each of them before he departed.

In Sy's office, Sy said, "I need to improve my ability to confront and talk through an issue."

Dave was reassuring. "You have come a long way. The important thing is that you have courage, are open, and you want to learn."

In Mack's office, Mack said, "What can I do? I understand my impact, but I need techniques to change." Dave gave the following counsel:

> Sy said that you go on too long and when he has had enough, he starts getting irritated. After you've talked a little bit, check with him. Help him stop you. Others have said, "You overpower me." Well, after a burst of your feelings, stop and ask for others to come back at you. Ask them whether you have come on too strong. Ask third persons to react. Give the other guy support.
>
> I've observed that you don't usually give a guy a handle. A guy challenges you. You come back at him, but very often you don't meet his point. It leaves a guy feeling helpless. Stop and ask yourself out loud: "Now, am I joining the issue?" Invite him to help you answer your own question.

Mack and Dave discussed these suggestions until Mack was satisfied that he understood what Dave was trying to say. In his discussion with the personnel manager, Dave urged him to take third-party roles, cautioning him that, as a member of the staff, he takes additional risks for himself.

Further Developments

Over the next six weeks following his visit to Indianapolis, Dave received a series of long-distance phone calls from members of the staff group.

Dave learned from the personnel manager, the director, and Mack that Sy and Mack were not actively working to improve their relationship. Instead Mack had concluded that his real conflict was with the director. Mack and the director were now seriously working on their conflict in an effort to reach a better understanding.

Mack mentioned several things which perhaps related to why he had not met with Sy. (1) He observed that the less he talked in meetings, the more Sy talked, as if Sy was simply relieved to have Mack withdraw, and "to have the show to himself." (2) Mack reported being rebuffed by Sy twice, once regarding a task contribution and the second time in a more interpersonal context. (3) Mack said he now realized that Sy, as assistant director, was only doing what the director wanted, anyway. It was the director, not Sy himself, who decided that Sy would take over the X Mill project that Mack was so disappointed to lose.

Still other inferences can be drawn from the situation. Perhaps Mack decided to work on his relationship with the director because it was the more crucial for his career. The director, himself, had a tendency to try to work on his *own* relationships with his subordinates, rather than on their relationships with each other. Apparently Mack clearly resented what he regarded as the director's close supervisory style; and the director, in turn, had been threatened by Mack's aggressive style.

Reconciliation

In follow-up consultation six weeks later, Sy stated that he had not met with Mack because of his preoccupation with the X Mill project and the discomfort he experienced whenever he dealt with him. Nevertheless, he wanted to meet with Mack and the consultant again.

Mack explained to Dave that the feedback he had received first from Sy and then from the director had prompted him to adjust his style of working. He and Dave discussed the nature of these adjustments and the associated personal costs. He wanted to meet with Sy, if the latter was interested.

The three of them went for lunch. Initially, Dave was not sure what use Sy and Mack would want to make of this meeting. It soon became evident that both wanted to deal with their relationship and other matters of personal significance.

Mack began talking about his internal dilemmas, how he had coped with them, the personal costs involved for him, his willingness to suffer his problem, and the career choices that might be approaching — most of which he had not discussed with others on the staff. Mack shared the following inner thoughts.

He had developed a staff concept to help him resist his

tendency to be domineering. He was desperately trying to live up to the model. First, he wanted to learn how to increase others' alternatives, to present issues in a way that did not prejudice them, and to avoid imposing his own views. Second, he was determined not to inject himself into situations unless someone consulted him or invited him. Because he was only infrequently invited to participate, this confirmed that others, including Sy, were relieved to have him off their backs. He felt underappreciated and rejected. But as unsatisfactory as this was for him personally, he believed that this staff pattern was better for the management group as a whole. Third, he expressed genuine interest in the welfare and task performance of others, and especially for Sy's work on the X Mill project.

Mack then described how he was currently coping with the mismatch between others' expectations of him and his own personal needs. In struggling against his natural tendency to invest himself enthusiastically in a job, probably more thoroughly than most managers, he was attempting to make a measured but adequate investment in the controller's job. This involved fighting another tendency to completely withdraw, a matter of central significance in his relationship with Sy.

Mack finally talked about his personal career alternatives. The net personal cost for him to live by the staff concept was large and he was pursuing other job possibilities. He had come to the conclusion that he was effective as a promoter, a one-man show. He could get along with superiors and subordinates, but not peers. Maybe he would find a job where peer relations were not important.

Dave had learned some of these feelings and thoughts from his earlier discussion with Mack. Therefore, he could both encourage and assist Mack in verbalizing his feelings. Sy was silent throughout and did not make a verbal response when Mack had finished. Dave's own observations convinced him that Sy had been listening empathically to Mack and was moved. Mack, however, had revealed feelings, thoughts, explanations, and prospects that were of personal significance. Now he appeared to be anxious about Sy's response or the lack of a specific response.

Dave asked Sy to share his current feelings and thoughts — to respond to Mack. Sy expressed feelings of understanding and compassion for Mack and sincere appreciation of Mack's concern for Sy's welfare. He also recognized Mack's interest in being directly helpful to him. He acknowledged that Mack was accurate in his perception that he (Sy) preferred a "middle-of-the-road" type of staff pattern. Sy said he could neither cope with Mack when the latter was at full throttle nor accept him when he withdrew completely.

Sy continued to talk thoughtfully. He said, "I find I do prefer to deal with [a subordinate of Mack's] on controller matters rather than with you." Mack's response was, "Beautiful!" The exclamation was spontaneous and vigorous, as if the authenticity of Sy's remark about his preference to work with Mack's subordinate was necessary to make Sy's earlier statement of compassion and understanding for Mack fully credible. Dave was also struck by the combination of sympathy and toughness in Sy's response to Mack's revelations of his internal dilemmas. Mack went on to request Sy's support for a promotion he was seeking for the subordinate in question. The promotion would ensure that he would be Mack's successor.

The long encounter over lunch was a very emotional experience, a type of reconciliation between Sy and Mack. They had experienced an emotionally moving self-disclosure, reciprocated by an expression of deeply felt concern. This contrasted with the basic antagonism expressed in the earlier confrontation. They had now expressed mutual concern for one another's welfare. While their respective styles kept them from wanting to work with each other, their negative feelings had been replaced by a form of positive feelings. Dave's prediction was that they might yet be able to develop a working relationship.

The third-party consultant was less active than in the earlier encounter, but his presence had clearly provided the impetus and the reassurance necessary for the principals to meet again.

Outcome

Within the next few weeks, Mack and the director worked through their differences and reached a mutually satisfying and productive relationship. When the consultant visited two months later, Mack had developed a satisfactory and satisfying outlook on life and work. Finally, the consultant also observed two long meetings of business appraisal and planning in which Sy and Mack worked intensively with each other, and they worked effectively.

Thus over the four-month period covered by this case study, the relationship between Sy and Mack had improved markedly. In the beginning it was negative on two counts: it greatly interfered with their current work, and it was a liability in terms of future career prospects. At the end of the period, the relationship was satisfactory (not exceptional) on both counts.

The series of encounters reported here, in which the third party played a central role, were instrumental in producing this change. During the period between the confrontation and the reconciliation, there were changes affecting Mack individually, which also created the potential for a change in the relationship. However, the principals did not really work together by themselves, and certainly did not make progress on their relationship. If anything, Mack had become discouraged by the failure of his minor attempts to resume a dialogue on their relationship.

As it turned out, the burden of behavior change had fallen on Mack. He had formulated his choice as "adapt somewhat or leave," and neither was easy for him. Dave, concerned about the personal costs that Mack might incur in forgoing his assertiveness, had provided support for his search for a new position. A modest search effort had not produced a satisfactory alternative for Mack and his family. Moreover, Mack had a positive interest in developing an ability to work effectively with peers, even if that involved throttling this aggressiveness. It should be reported that Mack's change was not absolute. Later he was able to resume his aggressiveness in ways that did not interfere with the functioning of others. Within two years both men were promoted — to positions elsewhere in the firm.

4

Fred–Charles

Searching for an Accommodation

The episode reported here involved two managers of a division of a large firm. Their dialogue involved clarifying their differences in an effort to find more accommodating interpersonal and staff–line relationships. The third party's interventions were more active than those in the two preceding cases.

Background

Charles, personnel manager, and Fred, production superintendent, both reported to the division's general manager. Dave, who acted as a third party, had worked as a consultant to the general manager's staff periodically over the past few years.

Sources of Stress on the Principals

About six months earlier, Charles had been promoted from another division to his present job. His performance had not yet met the expectations of the general manager, who had discussed this matter with him. One specific criticism was that unlike his predecessor, Charles was not functioning as an internal consultant and counselor. Charles considered this function less important than certain other personnel functions that he thought had been neglected by his predecessor.

Charles was criticized for his handling of union relations. The general manager believed he was unnecessarily suspicious toward the union. Division managers were proud of the accommodative relationship that they had developed with the union president, whom they regarded as trustworthy. Charles had not been directly responsible for labor relations in his previous job; nevertheless, he had been in a department with very antagonistic union relations.

Fred had been promoted recently to superintendent. While a few persons had some difficulty in getting along with him, he also was highly regarded by other associates and had the confidence of the general manager. He was assumed to be coping effectively with the constant pressure to solve new problems and improve performance. Of the two principals, Fred enjoyed more organizational support.

Their organizational relationship was important. Although both were interested in improving their relationship, the personnel manager had the greater objective need to improve it. By far the majority of employees served by the personnel department were in the superintendent's unit. To operate effectively Charles and his department must be accepted by Fred and his department. In fact, Fred's ties with the union president made it necessary for Charles to get along with Fred in order to develop a relationship with the union president.

Because they were new to the general manager's staff, both principals had had only moderate contact with Dave before the episode reported here. Charles understood what Dave was trying to do, knew about some of the types of functions he performed, and presumably had developed trust and confidence in him. Fred apparently was reassured by the fact that several close colleagues and two superiors had placed their confidence in him.

Fred's Views of the Developing Conflict

Late on a Friday afternoon the consultant received a phone call from Fred:

> I'm calling you about Charles, especially as a result of a meeting today. Our relationship is not what it's got to be. I

> don't know what the trouble is . . . I think he doesn't trust me, the way I run my department. I've tried to share this with him. . . . He feels I've rejected his offer of service and I can see how he might construe it that way.
>
> Today we were talking about a fifth-step grievance. It concerned absenteeism, where we in production admittedly have done a poor job. So what he comes up with is, "Well, you know, I've offered help five times and you haven't taken us up on it." I said, "Crap, that's an oversimplification." I acknowledged the truth, but resented the patness of his answer. Tied in with this is a hidden gripe, which is that I'm running the department five people short, in part because Personnel has not gotten me the people. Therefore, I'm annoyed at getting pat answers.
>
> The fact is that we have not placed priority on absenteeism. . . . But he [Charles] sits in a comfortable position. . . . It's easy for him to throw darts.
>
> I told him, "Yes, we should have invited you in, but your hands are not so clean . . . and I resent the excessive criticism." We need to sit down and work on this.

Dave asked Fred how he felt now about this interchange with Charles. Fred replied:

> I shared so much that I'm embarrassed. The meeting included the general manager, the chief engineer, and one of Charles's subordinates. I'm sorry about Charles's subordinate being there.

Dave asked Fred whether he and Charles had disagreed on how to handle the grievance. Fred answered:

> Yes. He was very suspicious of the union president and wanted to hold back on something the rest of us thought was fair.
>
> As a matter of fact, I, too, locked horns with the union president intially when he took over. At first, he saw things as black and white; but now he sees them as gray, and we have developed trust.
>
> In any event, when Charles came, I had been sharing things with the union president. Charles said that some-

> thing I'd just done was unwise, that it might lead to a side agreement. Well, I blew my stack, because I have better judgment than that. . . . As it turns out, I see Charles going through some of the same things with the union president that I did. I just hope he works through to an understanding. The union president came to me and we talked about this grievance. I related this conversation and requested Charles to take the union president at his word.

Dave offered that it seemed "pretty understandable" that Charles would resent the close relationship between Fred and the union president. Fred answered:

> That's true, but if he doesn't trust me, I'm teed off.
>
> Also, shortly after he arrived, there was a salary meeting in which he [Charles] talked in circles. I didn't think he could talk straight, but now I believe he can do better than he did then.
>
> The question is, why doesn't he trust me? But when I put it on the table that way, he says, "What makes you believe that?"
>
> It bothers me, it grinds me, that he can get to me so quickly. Not that he tries to. I don't have that kind of relationship with anyone else here. . . . I ought to be able to be cool and philosophical. There is no personal animosity. He's a nice wholesome guy . . . a regular fellow . . . nothing personal involved . . . we don't socialize outside business.

Dave asked Fred to think out loud about the ways in which his own relationship with the union president might be a factor in Charles's attitude. Fred responded:

> As I went into the grievance meeting, I said, "I agree with the union president." When Charles challenged my ability to predict what the union would do, I also said, "I've got the best relationship with the union president . . . I think I can feel him out before the meeting." Charles's response was that any meeting before the fifth step might dilute the fifth step. I answered, "I've already met him." . . . Yes, this could be threatening to Charles. However, the union

president wants to develop a good relationship with the personnel manager as well as with the production superintendent.

Charles's View

The following Wednesday, Dave talked by phone with Charles, who reported the following:

> I had an emotional meeting with Fred last Friday. It resulted from my strong concern with absenteeism and tardiness. A few months ago I had identified a mounting cost problem. I had said to Fred, "Hey, who is worrying about this?" Fred answered, "I'll have my two production supervisors go to work on it." I said, "Can I help?" He said, "No." Two weeks later I asked how it was going, and again he reassured me. This happened three more times. Finally we had a grievance, which I think could have been avoided. A supervisor cracked down too hard without tightening up in advance gradually and with warnings.
>
> Monday morning I talked with Fred, identifying our conflict. It may not be more important than a working relationship. I felt the pressing need to go to work on the absenteeism problem. I said, "I didn't want to undercut your position by working with your men without your permission." He said, "Go ahead and work on the problems you see." Therefore, I believe it's at least partly resolved.
>
> Maybe [the chief engineer] has talked with him, urging him not to simply get the bit in his teeth and go charging off without worrying about implications for others.
>
> I had a warm feeling for [the chief engineer] on Saturday morning. He said, "Let me know if I can help. I like both of you too well to let you guys get into trouble with each other."
>
> I believe there is a fringe benefit of my confronting Fred, because it took place with [the general manager and the chief engineer] present. I hope the general manager, especially, can see me other than reserved. This incident revealed my willingness to take some risks, which he has been urging me to do.

Immediately before his dialogue with Fred, Charles told Dave that at least three others had had trouble in trying to work with Fred at one point or another, indicating that he was reassured it was not simply his (Charles's) problem.

The Principals' Relationships with Other Staff Members

Dave's understanding of the relations among the members of the staff is sketched in Figure 4–1, which indicates that the

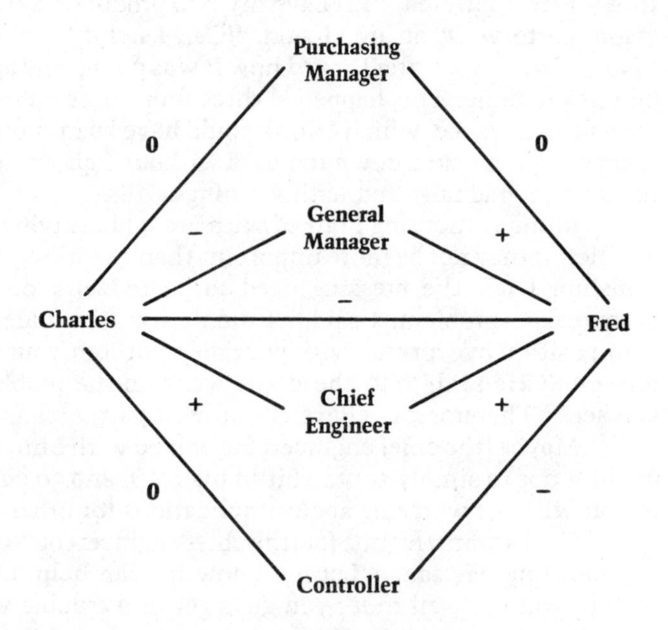

Key
+ indicates a positive mutual trust relationship
– indicates a low trust relationship
0 denotes an indifferent or ambivalent relationship

Figure 4–1
Relationship of Staff Members with Fred and Charles

chief engineer was the only staff member who had positive relations with both principals and might serve as an internal third party.

An Illustrative Conflict

The consultant spent the first half day of a two-day visit to the division observing and assisting in the critique of the general manager's staff meeting. The following interchange occurred between Fred and Charles. The latter suggested that the management decision on hours and scheduling might involve certain labor relations risks — either a union charge of a lockout or a vigorous attempt in the next negotiations to get a contract provision restricting management's flexibility.

Fred (referring to Charles's concerns): That is a very judgmental thing. I intend to lobby to the very bitter end not to run that overtime shift.

The general manager (interjecting): I know it is a matter of judgment and I don't know how to weigh the risk, but it should be considered . . . can I hear from you and Charles on this? (The implication was that he wanted them to get together outside of staff meeting and then report to him.)

Fred (continuining to pursue the matter, implying that the decision was an instance of a more general issue): I think we ought to make this decision by the numbers. We can't give here and there. The point is we need to run this plant as it should be run.

Charles (retorting): Bear in mind that the worst thing that could happen by running by the numbers is a lockout. There are some potential problems from a labor relations point of view. Let me dig into this.

The general manager: Both of you dig into this.

The boss attempted to ensure that the two would meet, discuss the matter, and report to him. Also, he achieved some neutrality vis-à-vis the principals first by urging Fred to consider Charles's views and then by prompting Charles not to go off on his own.

Decision to Work on the Fred–Charles Conflict

Dave had avoided any decision in advance of the staff meeting about how his time would be used over the next day and a half. Several individual staff members had expressed an interest in spending time with him, in some cases alone, in other cases with another member of the staff, and in still other cases with one or more subordinates. Dave wanted to resist trying to respond to more than a few of these, and he wanted the choices to be made in the staff group context. He also wanted to make it possible to replan on the basis of developments.

At the end of the meeting, the staff critiqued their meeting. Several organizational difficulties were also identified and discussed. Then Dave asked group members to consider how he should plan to use the next day and a half.

The plan was for Dave to meet with others during lunch and immediately after lunch, and then get together with Charles and Fred about 3:30 P.M. That meeting "could run over into dinner, if necessary." This open-ended arrangement was probably the most conducive to a good dialogue between Charles and Fred. The consultant was to participate in a task group's meetings the following day.

Of what significance to the Fred–Charles dialogue itself was the manner in which it was planned? Some possibilities can be suggested. Each person was given an explicit opportunity to express his interest, or lack of interest, in meeting. If he was reluctant to meet, it was possible to signal this in a variety of subtle ways (for example, by holding back, by finding it difficult to agree upon a meeting time, by sidetracking the discussion). Also, the discussion leading to this decision showed this particular pair the extent to which other staff members gave priority to the resolution of their differences.

Confrontation: Differentiation Phase

Getting the Issue on the Table

The session was started by Dave suggesting that Fred and Charles continue their discussion of the disagreement raised during the staff meeting. They agreed, and proceeded to do so. Thus the third party could observe their pattern of interaction, hear their stated positions, and listen for their underlying concerns before he needed to be more active.

It soon became clear that Charles was not necessarily opposed to the decision urged by Fred. He wanted to "reserve judgment" until he received the advice of a lawyer and corporate personnel. Fred, on the other hand, felt that Charles was being unduly cautious, asserting that even a production manager like himself could see that the decision obviously would *not* have the labor relations implications Charles was alluding to. He thought the scheduling decision could be made "tentatively," and then, if Charles learned something that made him believe the decision was unwise, it could be discussed. Inasmuch as the decision affected schedules three weeks hence, and Charles could get his advice within a couple of days, there were no urgent *action* implications of the issue. Nevertheless, the disagreement appeared to be relevant to their general interpersonal and staff–line conflict.

After some time, and just as the debate appeared to have become repetitive, Dave attempted to shift their attention to the more general form of the issue. He asked:

> Is this specific decision just an occasion for you to work on your differing views about the role of the personnel manager? I see you, Charles, using this to make the point that whenever there might be labor relations implications you believe you should be consulted, and that Fred should not rely upon his own unilateral judgment about the importance of potential labor relations implications. Am I right that you feel you have trouble with Personnel being ignored along these lines?

Turning to Fred, Dave continued,

> Fred, I see you saying that the decision is obvious and that you are annoyed with Charles for making a jurisdictional issue out of it. If that is correct, is it a common pattern?

The discussion that followed confirmed that these were significant themes in their disagreements.

Identifying Stylistic Differences

Then, somewhat later, Fred noted how he and Charles were different. Picking up this idea, Dave suggested that each share his views of how their personal styles differed. During the discussion that followed, Fred and Charles displayed the constrasts set forth in Figure 4–2.

After both had revealed their perceptions, Fred added another difference: he saw himself as taking people and issues at face value, whereas Charles was "probing, distrustful, doubtful,

Fred	**Charles**
Fred saw himself as	**Fred saw Charles as**
Direct	Indirect, using hidden meanings, meandering, hypothetical
Dealing in "black and white"	Treating everything as "gray"
A shirt-sleeves, stevedore type	
Relying upon personal relationships	Scholarly, professional, cap and gown
Decisive, "Laying matters on the table to look at them"	Insisting upon formal organizational channels
	Indecisive, hesitant, cautious, "Sorting things out into separate piles"
Charles saw Fred as	**Charles saw himself as**
Impulsive	Looking ahead
Not thorough	Thorough
Not caring whom he made problems for; not considering his effect on others	More considerate

Figure 4–2
The Principals' Perceptions of Themselves and Each Other

assuming a credibility gap, conjuring up problems." Fred had become more emotional. From time to time, at Dave's urging, he had expressed the feelings he experienced as a result of Charles's style; he felt himself "seething," "ground," "strained to the limit." Fred also believed that Charles got "bothered" and "bent out of shape" in reaction to him. Fred had been allowed to predominate in this discussion because he evidenced greater urgency in setting these types of perceptions out on the table.

In turning to hear more from Charles, Dave reviewed all of Fred's perceptions of him, enabling Charles to respond to an issue that was relatively important to him, rather than simply the most recent one mentioned by Fred.

Charles objected to Fred's charge that he tended to be distrustful toward others, saying that Fred could never give him specific instances. Thereupon, Fred related the fifth-step grievance episode and asserted that Charles's approach to the union reflected unduly low trust. It developed that the two disagreed completely in their recollection of these events.

During this discussion, the consultant noted a pattern in Charles's behavior that appeared to irritate Fred and add to his tension. It was also irritating to Dave. Charles had a tendency to ask a leading question that either forced an admission of fault or revealed inconsistencies. It was an examining style. Over the next hour, Dave made four types of attempts to call attention to this pattern, and modify it, or nullify its adverse effects.

First, Dave called attention to the cross-examination style and asked Fred how he was reacting to it. Fred confirmed his resentment. Thus, Charles had more information about how others react to this pattern of his.

Second, and in connection with the above intervention, Dave shared what his own reaction to this style would be, if he were the person being cross-examined. He used a hostile, graphic gesture.

Third, at a later point, Dave stopped the continuing attempt to reconstruct what had happened at the fifth-step meeting (where there were very contradictory recollections of events), and asked, "What would each of you be inclined to do with this difference?" Their responses dramatically illustrated one of their differences: Fred was inclined to drop it as not being productive.

Charles was inclined to get a witness, cross-examine him, and take any step required in order to determine who was correct. When Charles reflected upon this difference, he gained some insight into his own pattern. He also acknowledged it might not always be productive.

Then, Charles, who had had less opportunity to state what he didn't like about Fred's behavior, added an item.

Charles: Fred, you lack humility.

Fred: And do you want to teach it to me?

Dave: Charles, do you see *yourself* as having humility?

Charles: Yes.

Dave: Fred, do you see Charles that way?

Fred: It's *false* humility.

Charles then cited his earlier admission that he lacked the knowledge to make a judgment on the labor relations implications of the scheduling issue. He indicated that this was humility. Fred disagreed with that interpretation. He observed that this "admission of lack of knowledge" was tactical to Charles's purposes and didn't strike him as humility.

Later, Fred sharpened one source of resentment toward Charles. He saw Charles as doubting the judgment of production management on labor relations matters, and acting as if he were "saving production people from their own transgressions," as if he were "standing at the pass."

Escalation of Personal Attacks

Still later, they discussed a recent exchange between them. Fred had observed that the price of cartons of milk in the canteen had been increased. Profits from the canteen went to the recreation fund, which had more money than it needed. Therefore, he had mentioned his disapproval of the price increase to a member of Personnel. The two principals began rehashing the incident in an escalating tone.

Charles: My subordinates said to me, "Boy, are we in bad shape if our production superintendent doesn't have anything better to do than second guess us on the price of milk."

Fred: That's defensive. It's not clear you had a good reason. The price of milk affects everyone. Only a few benefit from the recreation fund.

Charles: You are being defensive. You are the only one in the plant who has complained about the price of milk. What does that tell you?

Fred: Somebody has to speak up. For example, to cite another instance, if I hadn't called your attention to the bad trash situation people would still be stepping over it day after day. It's funny, the cafeteria is the only thing you have to manage. (Fred was making the point that unlike the personnel department, Production continuously has to make decisions and take action, and therefore becomes vulnerable to criticism. This asymmetry had been a source of discomfort to Fred. Here, in the milk incident, he appeared to be trying to achieve more symmetry in this respect.)

Charles: If you would like to run the cafeteria we'd be happy to let you take it.

Dave cut off the discussion at this point. He indicated that it was 6:25 P.M. and that the chief engineer who was to join them for drinks had expected them to come by his office about a half hour earlier. Although Dave did not formulate it in his mind at the time, another reason favoring the termination of the discussion at that point was that it had degenerated to personal attacks, which seemed to intensify the mutual antagonism, rather than clarify basic issues.

Partly in order to provide some closure on the discussion, Dave summarized the "essential point" of each of the principals, and indicated that each had an understandable view:

> The discussion of the milk incident has been somewhat repetitive. Let me try to state the points each of you are making, as I hear them. Fred is saying, "Why should you get upset if I bring to your attention the idea that it doesn't make sense to increase the price of milk when the funds aren't all being spent now." He is saying to you, Charles, "Can't you accept this idea on its merit?" I believe I can understand Fred's sentiment here.
>
> On the other hand, Charles is saying to you, Fred, "This criticism is symbolic of your attitude to us, of your

tendency to get involved in our area, and we resent it. It's as if you *wanted* to find fault — and it's this general attitude that bothers us." That, too, I must admit, is an understandable view.

Am I right? That is, did I capture your essential points? (Both agreed.)

Apparently such a summary statement by the third party increased their respective feelings of being understood, and also avoided the question of which of them was going to have the last word in that interchange. In addition, Dave overlooked the more personal and more destructive attacks and counterattacks that both had used in tactical support of stating and supporting their "essential points." It might have been more helpful for Dave to have noted these tactics and helped the parties to understand how this type of interchange had developed or degenerated. This might have been an excellent way for Dave to differentiate between constructive and destructive dialogue. This opportunity was clear to him only on hindsight.

Continuing the Dialogue for New Insights

The chief engineer joined them and they went to a restaurant for drinks and dinner. They worked until 11:30 P.M.

The chief engineer had joined the group at the consultant's invitation and with the concurrence of Charles and Fred. Although he was relatively inactive, he made several important contributions. First, he asked the group to help him think through a specific decision he had to make concerning a subordinate. The group responded and discussed this with him. Second, when asked at one point for his reactions to what was going on between Fred and Charles, he gave them a common, blunt reaction, namely, "I think you guys are both lecturing each other." After that comment, they both dug in and dealt with each other more directly. Third, his presence limited their tendencies to use "unfair" tactics and provided the prospect of being available to them in the future, either individually or as a pair.

The following discussion focuses on the consultant's actions, first describing the intervention in an abstract way, and then illustrating it.

Analyzing the Ongoing Process

An interesting interchange illustrates the power of analyzing the ongoing interaction. Fred, the production superintendent, turned to Dave after a lull in the discussions.

Fred: Dave, it's a little off the current subject, but I want to get your reaction to an idea. I've been talking with the union president about what you've been doing with the management staff and he is intrigued and interested. You know he likes to develop his own abilities . . . I was wondering what your ideas are about spending an hour or so with him?

Dave: By posing that question to me, you've created a dilemma for me. It's an interesting idea and I do want to respond to it, but, if I do, we will have created additional problems in your relationship with Charles. Have you checked the idea with Charles? (Fred indicated that he had not.) My guess is that right now he's sitting here feeling excluded, bypassed, and is getting riled up. This is an instance when you are not recognizing him as the personnel manager.

Fred: My gosh, I see what you mean. It was unconscious. It never occurred to me I was excluding or bypassing Charles.

Gaining a Differentiated View of the Other Person

Dave called attention to what he perceived as important variations in a person's behavior during the period of their discussions. Then he would check with the second person to see whether he perceived the same variations. In some cases, one type of behavior had been negatively reacted to, and the other behavior had been positively received. Dave would press to achieve as much insight into these distinctions as possible. An illustration follows.

Recall that earlier in the dialogue Fred had said that Charles showed "a false humility." He had said that when Charles admitted he didn't know something, the admission was tactical, to buy time. Later in the day, there was an instance where Charles was "piling on," was showing delight at the fact that Fred had been brought up short by one of the consultant's observations. Dave confronted Charles with the idea that he had just "piled on." Charles appreciated the point. His face flushed and he said, "I'm sorry . . ." "I regret that . . . I don't like that [in myself]." However, Fred appeared to completely ignore these statements of regret or sentiments of shame expressed by Charles.

Since Dave believed there had been something very different about Charles's expression of humility in these two instances, he confronted Fred, and said, "I want to check something out with you. What did Charles just say and was it another instance of 'false humility'?" Fred said that he did *not* feel it was false in this instance. In effect, Dave gave maximum opportunity for Fred to reinforce Charles's behavior in the second instance. More important, the intervention acknowledged to Charles that he was perceived in one way one time and in another way a second time.

The Parties' Expectations

The consultant counseled the parties to anticipate disappointments in the course of trying to build a relationship. Consider the following interchange:

Charles: At some point the whole thing will click. I feel we will have an excellent relationship. (This was said in an enthusiastic way.)

Fred: It's not that easy. I see it as a process of being open about how we interfere with and grind each other, and gradually being more accommodative.

Dave: I guess I see it much as Fred does. In part, it's because guys like you, Charles, generally find it much easier to get along with guys like Fred than vice versa.

Dave also pointed out the rejection potential for Charles in the foregoing. Charles acknowledged that he had felt immediate rejection. The parties were alerted to this problem of rejection. They discussed whether it was possible to take the sting out of future "overtures not reciprocated." As a result of this interchange, Charles might in the future be more likely to talk directly with Fred about the effect of such rejection, rather than to counterattack in an indirect way.

Similarities Between the Principals

The consultant identified similarities between the parties, especially as they referred to instances occurring in the interaction (the patterns of lecturing, scolding, preaching, condescending, helping, or informing). The following illustrates the point:

Fred had effectively made a point of Charles's lecturing, pointing out that, not only did he see Charles this way, but his subordinates did too. Fred had said, "You act as if it's your job to point out mistakes, how people went wrong, but not to work to prevent problems in advance."

Much later the chief engineer said, "You're both lecturing each other." Dave agreed and pointed out to Fred that he usually preceded a lecturing bit with the words, "You see . . ." Dave provided several illustrations from the past hour. Fred fully registered the feedback and said he hadn't even realized that he was using the words "You see."

Common Goals

Dave identified a goal where they might really go astray if they had not worked things out by then: resolving management's priorities on items in labor negotiations. This and other third-party actions are illustrated by the following interchange:

Fred: I want to make sure my two subordinates have a say about the items that go forward to the corporate office.

Charles: I intend to provide that opportunity.

Fred: (Made a very divisive, challenging statement about the amount of control he wanted for line versus staff.)

Charles: (Made a statement to the effect that the line would have influence, but would not have final say.)

Fred: (Referred to "unanimity.")

Charles: It's unrealistic to state in advance that all of the decisions will be unanimous.

Fred: Well, perhaps this has become hypothetical.

Dave: Yes, but why? I see you in this instance as feisty; as if you were looking for ways to challenge Personnel, especially Charles. . . . I'm afraid that unless you guys have worked this through, the management discussions prior to labor negotiations are going to involve more conflict than the negotiations themselves. . . . An initial difference of opinion will become exaggerated and polarized. (Then, turning to the chief engineer:) I rather hope you get involved—as a sort of neutral guy—in the preliminary discussions.

Charles (chiming in): That's why *I* said I wanted you involved.

Dave (glowering at Charles): There's a difference in what I said and what you said. I saw him [the chief engineer] as a neutral. I see you as making a bid for a coalition, or for using my statement against Fred.

This interchange illustrates several other third-party interventions. First, Dave identified the chief engineer as a third party, legitimating his behavior in this role and coordinating expectations for him to play this role in a particular future situation. Second, Dave disassociated himself from, and "punished" Charles for, an act that appeared to have the intent of putting Fred down.

Outcomes from the Confrontation

What were the prospects for resolving the substantive and emotional conflicts in the Fred–Charles case? Their respective role expectations did involve substantial disagreement; however, these differences presumably could be partly compromised and partly integrated, provided the two could develop some positive interpersonal rapport.

During the six months they had known each other, their encounters had been only moderately intensive; the resultant interpersonal resentments were genuine, but did not appear to be so strong that they could not be worked through. Finally, while their personal styles (indirectness, impulsivity) might be expected to be the basis of irritation, they did not seem to be significant enough to prevent interpersonal accommodation.

In conclusion, the conflict appeared to be amenable to resolution or better control. If the differences in their respective labor relations philosophies and role definitions had been more basic, then dialogue and process interventions of the type described here would have limited potential. In that case, solutions would require change in personnel or organization structure.

If the jurisdictional issue could be worked through, there was the prospect for creative balance and synthesis of their respective orientations to labor relations and their styles of decision making. The jurisdictional issue would be less significant if the blaming pattern subsided; the blaming pattern, in turn, would be less obtrusive if the two were able to develop mutual respect and trust.

The confrontation that took place was without a high emotional climax; rather it was sustained at a moderate level of emotionality. There were periods in which the discussion became repetitive and circular, but on the whole there was a progressive movement to the interchange. For example, greater insights into one's own or the other's interpersonal patterns and personal concerns were first registered, later illustrated again by subsequent actions, and still later anticipated by one or both of the parties. Having a common understanding of these patterns and being able to anticipate them, they could learn to joke about them and perhaps to avoid the interaction pattern. Therefore, the pattern itself, which was mutually offensive, did not add "more fuel to the fire."

At the end of the day, each of the parties had more insight into what he was doing to promote the conflict, and each appeared to have *some* increased confidence in the positive intentions of the other. They had a little better understanding of the underlying emotional and organizational bases that were common to most of the substantive issues about which they found themselves in disagreement. It was not, however, apparent that their respect for each other had been greatly increased. They had learned about and practiced some ways of working on their misunderstandings that were probably more productive than those they had used previously. They had a common understanding of the difficulty and the time that would probably be involved in improving their relationship; that is, Charles became less hopeful of a short-run breakthrough, and Fred became more optimistic about eventually developing an accommodative pattern. There probably was higher commitment to improve the relationship and to engage in joint projects such as supervisory training. There was increased awareness of the future costs of not being able to manage their interpersonal conflict, particularly as it could affect preparation for labor negotiations a few months hence.

Both explicitly expressed satisfaction with the process and its results during the meeting. The next day Charles expressed feelings that they had made headway and yet clearly manifested some continued basic distrust of Fred. Fred, without saying just how his attitude or perceptions of Charles had changed, said that the day had been one of the most significant educational experiences in his life.

The confrontation itself increased the incentive to resolve their differences. First, there was a tendency for each of them to want to justify the time and energy invested in the effort to improve their relationship, and also to meet the expectations of other staff members. Second, the process underscored at least one more tangible area of interdependence, namely the approaching labor negotiations.

Although the confrontation had provided a basis and a start for reaching some working accommodation, Charles left the division and the corporation before the full effects of their efforts to build a relationship could be felt. The primary reason for his leaving was that he had not gained a relationship of mutual confidence with the general manager.

5

Diagnostic Model of Interpersonal Conflict

Interpersonal conflict is cyclical and the cycles may be either escalating, de-escalating, or maintaining of the level of conflict. A conflict cycle involves four basic elements: the issues, the circumstances that precipitate manifest conflict, the conflict-relevant acts of the principals, and the various consequences. Each of four strategies of conflict management relates to a different one of the four basic elements of the cyclical model. (See Table 5–1.)

Cyclical and Dynamic Characteristics

Interpersonal conflicts are *cyclical*. Two persons who are opposed are only periodically engaged in manifest conflict. At a point in time the issues between them may represent only latent conflict. Then, for some reason, their opposition becomes salient, the parties engage in a set of conflict-relevant behaviors, and they experience the consequences of the interchange. Then, once again, the conflict becomes less salient and less manifest for a time before the cycle repeats itself. (See Figure 5–1.)

Interpersonal conflicts also tend to be *dynamic*, that is to

Table 5–1
Conflict Dynamics and Conflict Management

	Purposes of Conflict Dialogue	
Elements of Conflict Cycle or Episode	**Diagnostic Objectives**	**Action Objectives**
1. Issues in conflict	Differentiate basic from symptomatic issues and resolvable from unresolvable issues	Resolve by compromise or integration of substantive differences and working through of emotional differences
2. Events or conditions that trigger manifest conflict	Identify barriers to conflict or conflict management behaviors and events that precipitate such behavior	Control by avoiding triggering new episode unless constructive purpose will be served
3. Manifest tactics or resolution initiatives	Understand how characteristic conflict behaviors can generate additional issues	Control by limiting destructive tactics, encouraging constructive initiatives
4. Consequences, including feelings produced by conflict	Understand the feelings generated by conflict episodes, how they are coped with, and therefore whether they are fueling the next episode	Control by assisting principals to cope better with feelings and other consequences of conflict

say, from one cycle to the next the issues or the form of the manifest conflict will typically undergo change. *Escalation* refers to a tendency for the relationship to become more conflictful. *Deescalation* refers to a trend toward less conflict (see Figure 5–2). If

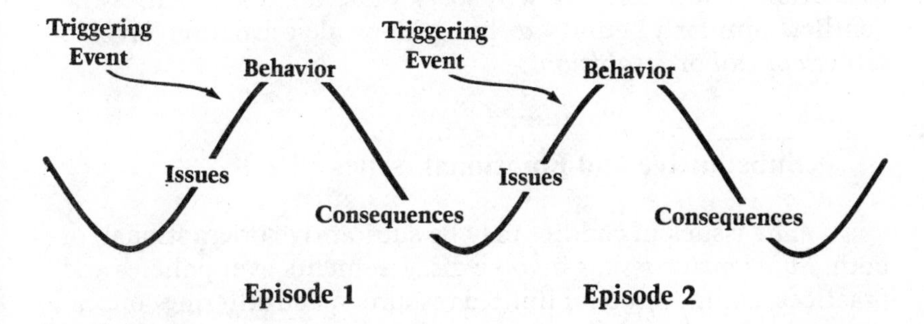

Figure 5-1
A Cyclical Model of Interpersonal Conflict

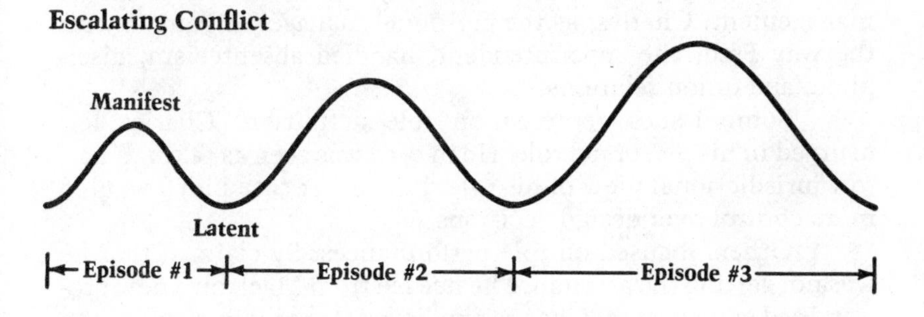

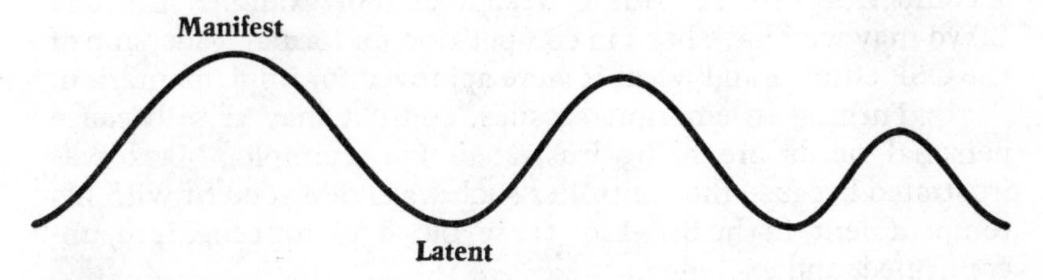

Figure 5-2
Escalating and De-escalating Patterns of Interpersonal Conflict

as a part of an overall strategy of conflict management temporary escalation is desirable, we will speak of acting to *de-control* the conflict. Similarly, efforts to bring about de-escalation involve either *control* or *resolution.*

Substantive and Emotional Issues

The issues in conflict may be substantive or emotional, or both. *Substantive issues* involve disagreements over policies and practices, competition for limited resources, and differing conceptions of roles. *Emotional issues* involve feelings such as anger, distrust, scorn, resentment, fear, and rejection.

Our three case histories contained several instances of differences about policies and practices. Sy disapproved of the controller's stronger orientation to headquarters than to the local management. Charles, as the personnel manager, disagreed with the way Fred, the superintendent, handled absenteeism, discipline, and union relations.

Some issues centered on role definition. Charles felt usurped in his personnel role. He in turn was seen as taking a narrow jurisdictional view of his role. In another case Lloyd wanted more control over design decisions.

Others focused on role performances. Sy claimed that he was not getting the assistance he needed from Mack on a new project. Fred believed that Charles as personnel manager provided too little assistance to manufacturing.

Another source of interpersonal conflict in organizations is a competition for rewards or resources. For example, Bill and Lloyd may well have been in competition for formal leadership of the OSP effort if and when it were approved for implementation.

Turning to emotional issues, conflict may arise because personal needs are being frustrated. For example, Mack was frustrated because the controller's job was not a good fit with his temperament. In the Bill–Lloyd case, Lloyd felt unrecognized, unconfirmed, and excluded.

Two persons may make contradictory personal demands on their relationship, based directly on their respective interpersonal needs. Mack's aggressiveness violated Sy's need to collaborate in a less highly charged atmosphere. Bill's personal preference for fluid, permissive relationships contradicted Lloyd's preference for more structure, clarity, and "crispness." Fred and Charles were each annoyed by the other's general personal style: Fred viewed Charles as academic, indirect, and cautious; Charles regarded Fred as impulsive and inconsiderate. Each perceived the other as lacking in humility and defensive.

Both substantive and emotional issues were involved in all three cases, although in differing degrees. In the Mack–Sy case the substantive issues paled in comparison with the personal issues. In the other two cases there was more balance between substantive and personal issues.

The distinction between substantive and emotional issues is important because the substantive conflict requires bargaining and problem solving between the principals and mediative interventions by the third party, whereas emotional conflict requires a restructuring of a person's perceptions and the working through of feelings between the principals, as well as conciliative interventions by the third party. The former processes are basically cognitive, the latter processes more affective.

Triggering Events

The interpersonal issues described above can exist as latent conflict for periods of time. The latent-manifest nature of interpersonal conflict is governed by the barriers to overt conflict actions and circumstances, which I call *triggering events,* which nevertheless overcome the barriers and precipitate actions.

A party may be deterred from confronting an interpersonal conflict by internal barriers such as attitudes, values, needs, desires, fears, anxieties, and habitual patterns of accommodating; and by external barriers, such as group norms against the expression of conflict, and physical obstacles to interaction. Examples of barriers include

- Task requirements (Time limits, for example, inhibit direct confrontation of feelings and issues involved in a conflict.)

- Group norms (Managers may believe they should not express negative feelings toward others.)
- Personal role concepts (A boss may feel that his ability to engage in conflict with a subordinate is limited by his supervisory role.)
- Public image (One may desire to maintain an image of gentility.)
- Perception of the other's vulnerability (The other person may be seen as too susceptible to hurt from a direct expression of feelings.)
- Perception of one's own vulnerability to the other's conflict tactics
- Fear that a conciliatory overture won't be reciprocated
- Physical barriers to interaction

Despite barriers such as the ones just named, some circumstances may be capable of starting a conflict cycle; they set off a round of hostile interactions, a vigorous disagreement, a candid confrontation, or a problem-solving interchange. A triggering event can have its effect either by increasing the salience of a conflict issue or by lowering a barrier to action. Parties may engage each other when a substantive issue becomes relevant to a required action. Or one may choose to explore the issue when the circumstances are especially favorable to one's position. Not surprisingly, where emotional issues are involved, the ignition of manifest conflict is explicable in less rational terms; offhand remarks and criticism on sensitive points are typical triggering events.

Thus, diagnosis of an interpersonal conflict involves discovering what types of barriers are customarily operating and what triggers the conflict cycle.

In the Bill–Lloyd case, barriers to direct mutual conflict were primarily internal to one party, namely Bill. He commented that without the consultant's presence he probably would not have confronted Lloyd "at the process level." Lloyd's strong, aggressive, interpersonal style intimidated Bill, who, as a result, avoided toe-to-toe exchanges with Lloyd in the larger group setting and procrastinated in confronting Lloyd outside the group.

The Bill–Lloyd case illustrates how conflict acts are easily triggered by a strong dose of the irritating condition, combined with a tempting tactical opportunity to put stress on the other person. The joint staff meetings exposed Lloyd directly to Bill's unstructured style and reminded him that Bill's was the single leadership role differentiated within the group, both of which irritated Lloyd. In this setting Lloyd could, by the same actions, differentiate himself within the total group and make Bill's life difficult. Besides, apparently Lloyd wanted to increase the stress on Bill in order to develop the latter's interest in reconsidering the status quo; the joint meetings afforded him an excellent opportunity to do just that.

The next question to address in this type of diagnosis of the Bill–Lloyd case is: What triggers a dialogue between participants who are managing so differently their respective sides of the conflict? Bill joined the conflict when he did because he felt mounting internal pressure and perceived new external support in the urgings of his superior and the availability of the consultant. During the confrontation meeting more specific circumstances encouraged Lloyd's openness about his feelings, a development that proved important in creating a positive cycle. These circumstances included the growing evidence that Bill and Dave were listening to, accepting, and responding to the issues he had already identified.

The Mack–Sy case contains similarities, but also contrasts. Like Bill above, Sy was inhibited by the other person's (Mack's) aggressive pattern. Apparently, Sy tended to suppress his anger and withdraw rather than show his feelings toward Mack or pursue his side of a disagreement. Like Bill, he joined the issue when the consultant was present. Sy's more spontaneous outburst at the staff meeting resulted from a combination of factors: he experienced mounting frustration at not having made headway on the dialogue, he perceived support from the presence of the consultant and other members of the staff, he had just witnessed a gross example of Mack's aggressiveness, and finally he had just suffered the criticism directed at an area of his responsibility.

It is significant that in this instance, despite his typically aggressive style, Mack did not really join the conflict issues in the two meetings during the consultant's first visit. He feared the potential adverse consequences for his future, he was already preoccupied with his current career dilemmas, and he may have perceived a tactical disadvantage since Sy had the initiative.

The Fred–Charles case illustrates a comparatively simple pattern. The significant barriers were the typical organizational norms against manifest conflict. Charles's organizational insecurity might have operated to some extent to inhibit him from completely opening up on Fred. However, Charles's conflict initiatives may have been encouraged by the presence of his boss, who had been urging him to take more risks in his relations with other departments, offsetting his inhibition based on his organizational insecurity. Apart from that indirect stimulus, either party was quick to engage the other whenever presented with an example of the other's behavior that he disliked. Therefore, Fred and Charles engaged in shorter and more frequent cycles of mutual conflict than the other two pairs.

Case-by-case analysis of barriers and triggering events suggests some possibilities for the constructive management of conflict.

First, it is important to choose the right issue, time, and place for joining the conflict. An understanding of barriers and triggering events helps this choice. To prevent manifest conflict, at least temporarily, one can reinforce the indicated barriers and attempt to head off the types of events that trigger manifest conflict. Conversely, if constructive dialogue is appropriate, one knows what barriers must be overcome and what factors will make the conflict especially salient for each principal. Because a different set of barriers and precipitating factors usually applies to each principal, one must find the circumstances that facilitate a mutual confrontation.

Second, for a particular interpersonal conflict, some events will trigger an escalating cycle and others a resolution effort. Diagnosis distinguishes between these two types of circumstances.

Third, an analysis of events that surround a conflict interchange often provides clues regarding the basic issues in the recurrent conflict.

Fourth, the frequency of conflict encounters may be

systematically controlled by operating on barriers and triggering events, a point discussed in a later section on the operational objectives of conflict management.

Conflict Tactics and Resolution Behaviors

Conflict becomes manifest by tactics and resolution overtures. They include expression of feelings — of conflict (anger, attack, avoidance, rejection) and of conciliation (regret, sympathy, warmth, support). They also include both the competitive strategies intended to win the conflict, such as blocking, interrupting, deprecating others, forming alliances, outmaneuvering the adversary, and one-upmanship; and the cooperative strategies intended to end the conflict, such as concessions and search for integrative solutions.

The potential costs and benefits of conflict include those that affect each of the participants personally (in psychological and career terms), their work, and others around them. These costs result from merely being in an antagonistic relationship, from the manifest tactics themselves, and from the reactions of others. Included in the costs of conflict are the missed opportunities for creative collaboration as well as more tangible consequences.

What if Bill and Lloyd had failed to ameliorate the situation in their case? The tension between them could have decreased the productivity of the OSP effort and increased employee turnover. One tactic of Lloyd's, his proposal to reassign personnel, had even more potential for escalating the conflict. If Lloyd had requested that some members of his professional staff be transferred permanently to Bill's group, he would have brought the unresolved conflict to the attention to their superiors. This development would have been embarrassing to one or both, and would have led to more intergroup maneuvering and more antagonism. At the same time such transfers did represent one solution to otherwise unresolved conflict: it would have reduced the intergroup interdependence and separated the main antagonists, Bill and Lloyd.

The case illustrates psychological costs paid by the participants — for Bill, personal disappointment if the total group's process reverted to an earlier pattern and harassment from a tough adversary, and for Lloyd, discomfort with Bill's style and exclusion from an opportunity to contribute and thereby experience enhanced self-worth.

The Bill–Lloyd case also illustrates plausible gains from conflict. Some level of rivalry between the two directors and their groups might enhance motivation, ensure a productive level of criticism, and increase the available number of alternative solutions to technical problems. Apparently, this productive level of tension would persist even if the major conflict issues between Bill and Lloyd were resolved. Psychologically, there were also potential gains. For example, Lloyd appeared rather to enjoy aspects of the interpersonal conflict, as if he were personally energized by it.

In the Mack–Sy case, the psychological cost of their interpersonal conflict was a dominant consideration. Sy had singled out his relationship with Mack as of special concern. Similarly, Mack had referred to the conflict as "intense" and was anxious about the risks to his career.

This conflict had surfaced only in the staff meeting when Sy had placed on the agenda the item "role of the controller." Prior to that the conflict had not come to the attention of other staff members. Although it had affected the work of Sy and Mack and thereby their respective areas, the conflict had had no particular importance for others.

Another potential cost had not materialized. In this organization a manifest, visible conflict between two aspiring managers could be costly to their careers. This was an especially important consideration for Sy, who felt he had to demonstrate interpersonal competence to his superiors and to himself. However, there was no basis for hypothesizing any gains to either party from the continuation of the conflict.

The confrontation and dialogue played a role in coordinating their efforts to resolve and/or control their conflict. After the conflict escalated to Sy's climactic outburst at the staff meeting, the conflict de-escalated. An early indication of a trend toward resolution was Mack's initial self-disclosures in the reconciliation session, suggesting that he was more confident of Sy's integrity. Their expressions of mutual concern during the consultant's second visit was a further step toward resolution. There was partial resolution and constructive control of the residual negative feelings, resulting in their ability to work effectively with each other. While the two men were not close friends, they were able to manage any continuing conflict.

The Fred–Charles conflict manifested itself in a range of behaviors, including fighting or arguing in front of others and criticizing, blaming, and lecturing each other. Charles, in particular, used a variety of conflict tactics. He used cross-examination; he showed pleasure when the consultant would confront Fred with some negative aspect of his behavior; and he attempted to ally himself with the consultant and the chief engineer.

The conflict affected performance. It sapped the energy of Fred and Charles and their associates. Differences of opinion were exaggerated and polarized. Issues like absenteeism which required joint effort were not being handled effectively.

Becoming embroiled in conflict with the manager of the major group his department served had implications for Charles's career. While this conflict was not the principal reason for his termination, and while the confrontation had provided encouragement that the conflict would be worked through, the fact is that this peer conflict may have hurt Charles's career.

The conflict had psychological costs and gains. Fred was embarrassed that he had lost his objectivity and felt guilty about "laying into" Charles in the presence of the latter's subordinates. Interestingly, the same confrontation included a fringe benefit for Charles, who was pleased at being able to demonstrate to the general manager a willingness to take risks.

Fred said he was "seething" and "strained to the limit" when confronted with Charles's interpersonal style. Charles, in turn, felt personally crowded and usurped whenever Fred would "get the bit between his teeth and go charging off without worrying about the implications for others." He felt excluded from the relationship between the superintendent and union president.

These descriptions of the principals' reactions do not indicate the magnitude of strain or stress that they experienced. The consultant judged the stress here to be less than that involved in the Mack–Sy case but more than that in the Bill–Lloyd case.

Moreover, both principals seemed relatively able to tolerate conflict and characteristically to enjoy a moderate level of conflict. Nevertheless, this contest was rather debilitating for both of them.

The tactics used by Fred and Charles tended to perpetuate or escalate the conflict. The criticizing and blaming exchanges were difficult to terminate because each wanted the last word. Derogation tactics had even more tendency to escalate. Fred asserted that even a production manager like himself could see that the decision in question obviously would *not* have the labor relations implications Charles was alluding to. In turn, Charles was deprecating in tone with his remark about the superintendent's not having anything better to do than second guess the personnel department on the price of milk. These remarks were taken as personal attacks.

What behaviors by Fred and Charles helped manage the conflict? They were fewer in number but included agreeing to meet and listening to each other; Charles's expressing regret for having gloated; Fred's acknowledging that Charles had made an authentic expression of regret; and Fred's nondefensive acknowledging of the fact that he had just bypassed Charles on a personnel department matter, once it was pointed out by the consultant.

Understanding the nature of conflict tactics is relevant to conflict management because conflict behaviors are the most available indexes of the existence of differences between persons and because the nature of the tactics largely determines the consequences of the conflict. Perhaps the most important diagnostic aspect of conflict management is an understanding of the consequences of an interpersonal conflict. The relevance is threefold.

First, do the costs of conflict outweigh the gains and do they justify the costs of mounting an effort to achieve a better management of the conflict?

Second, the analysis can indicate the connections between the conflict or conflict-management tactics that are used and the tendency for issues to proliferate or decrease in number.

Third, an understanding of the consequences of the current conflict combined with an appreciation of the issues involved, enables one to identify the outcomes that are desirable and realistic and to map general strategies for achieving the desired outcomes. Typically these involve strategies of de-escalation, whether through conflict control or conflict-resolution approaches.

Proliferation Tendencies

Of the issues identified with each of the three interpersonal conflicts, some would have developed earlier, others later. Diagnosis involves an attempt to assess which issues are more basic and which are more symptomatic, representing a proliferation of the basic issues. Issue proliferation occurs for a variety of reasons.

On the one hand, emotional conflict tends to create substantive disagreements that help the parties differentiate and separate themselves. Also, two parties may cooperate in using substantive issues to legitimate overt conflict; or one may use a substantive issue for tactical advantage.

On the other hand, substantive conflict may create emotional conflict, hostility, and lowered trust. If one disagrees with or competes with another, there is a psychological tendency to develop negative attitudes toward the other person. Moreover, the tactics of competition, debate, and bargaining over substantive differences contain many points of friction and are likely to result in feelings of being attacked, in perceptions that the other is unfair, and so on.

Whether the original and basic issue is substantive or emotional, the conflict is likely to develop additional issues symptomatic of both types. Thus, even though these three cases did not have long histories, by the time the parties confronted there existed many points of conflict. These issues were brought to the surface one by one; the principals and the third party continuously confronted choices of which issues to treat.

This tendency for one type of conflict to generate the other has several particular consequences. When emotional conflict causes parties to project substantive disagreements, they may be embarrassed to discover they are vigorously advocating positions about which they are basically uncertain or which may be inconsistent with other positions they have taken. Further, by locking in on substantive issues, they generate the possibilities for more tangible win–lose contests: this condition has its own perpetuation dynamics.

When substantive conflict produces emotional conflict, the latter creates "noise" in the communications upon which the parties must rely to confront the substantive issues. For example, if the most basic issues in the Fred–Charles conflict arose out of their differing conceptions of the staff–line relationship, the emergent distrust and ego-bruising exchanges virtually ensured that they could not work effectively on the substantive staff–line issues.

If two persons confront initially on symptomatic issues, they may decrease the costs of conflict, and create a climate favorable for dialogue on the more basic issues. However, it is helpful if *both* parties have an appreciation that the issues being dealt with are symptomatic. Otherwise, they are likely to have unrealistic expectations of harmony.

If the parties can gain an appreciation of how issues have been added on, they are better able to reconceive the present conflict in its more essential, original terms.

One of the purposes of dialogue between persons in extensive conflict with each other is to allow the parties to identify the more basic issues. In particular, the climate of acceptance in a dialogue setting influences whether a person will "own up to" his feelings, the nature of the emotions he has invested in the conflict. However, in fact the parties may de-escalate and even resolve their conflicts through dialogue without even clarifying between them precisely what issues were basic for each of them.

How to Manage Conflict

Let us continue to assume the conflicts are more dysfunctional than functional for the principals or others, and that there exists a desire to manage them more constructively. Typically, the most general objective is to interrupt a self-maintaining or escalating cycle and to initiate a de-escalating cycle. This objective applies whether the ultimate goal has been defined as control (minimizing the costs of the conflict without changing the basic issues in dispute) or resolution (eliminating the negative feelings and substantive disagreements).

Each element of a cycle suggests a measure of escalation and de-escalation, and identifies a corresponding target of conflict management (see Table 5-1). Three involve control; one requires resolution.

Prevent Ignition of a Conflict Interchange

One operational objective of conflict management might be to reduce the frequency of destructive conflictful encounters by strengthening the inhibitors to conflict actions and avoiding triggering events or blunting them when they occur. It is especially helpful to recognize early warning signals, signs that one or both parties are experiencing mounting stress.

In the Mack–Sy case, for example, certain aspects of the conflict could be controlled or avoided. If each found the other's style irritating (Sy complained that Mack was domineering; and Mack, that Sy was compulsive and detail oriented), each could attempt to overlook the behaviors involved and minimize their face-to-face contact. In fact, Sy attempted to terminate meetings with Mack when he became too agitated to continue. Also, Sy contacted Mack's subordinate rather than Mack personally whenever possible. Because there was a relatively steady turnover of personnel in the positions they currently held, it might have been feasible to attempt to merely "control" the conflict between these two men for the duration of their work relationship.

Generally, however, the drawback to control strategies that avoid conflict exchanges is that the eventual results may be less desirable than an early expression of the conflict:

1. The conflict may tend to go underground, become less direct but more destructive, and eventually become more difficult to confront and resolve.
2. The participants' suppression of the substantive issues and their antagonistic feelings may make the manifest conflict, when it does occur, more intense and destructive.

One difficulty with merely preventing manifest conflict, especially via barriers to expression of the conflict, is that they tend to prevent potentially constructive confrontations as well as other tactical exchanges. Nevertheless, these barriers can be utilized as a part of a more complex strategy—for example, to achieve a cooling-off period which will allow for other resolution initiatives or control efforts

Constrain the Form of the Conflict

The second operational objective does not try to prevent all conflict interchanges but attempts to set limits on the tactics employed. Sometimes substantive conflicts must be pursued according to the group norm that prescribes that if one criticizes the recommendation of another person, one must offer one's own recommendation. The rule prescribes that if you attack, you must likewise expose yourself by "stating your alternative." Thus, a certain symmetry is achieved in the offensive-defensive stances of those who disagree.

Acts based on emotional conflicts are also sometimes the subject of certain proscriptions and prescriptions. A social system may attempt to inhibit interpersonal conflict acts that occur in the presence of bosses or subordinates, because they are assumed to increase the cost of the conflict without serving any constructive purpose. Norms may attempt to rule out the tactics of "interpersonal billiards" whereby one principal attacks the other through some third person. Similarly, the group may be sensitive about "ganging up" on an individual, and, therefore, outlaw two-on-one interpersonal-conflict situations. In some systems it develops that one of the few permissible forms of expressing interpersonal antagonism is via humor, because the tension-raising attack is accompanied by its own tension-release act and therefore usually does not result in mutual conflict engagements that are feared.

As a control strategy, constraining the form of the conflict can be used in various ways: (1) to protect a social system from the disruptive consequences of less restrained conflict, and (2) to prevent a conflict from escalating by ruling out tactics more likely to be provocative.

Cope Differently with the Consequences of Conflict

The third operational objective minimizes the costs of a given set of conflict acts. Coping techniques influence not only the current psychological costs but also the proliferation tendencies. First, ventilating one's feelings to a friend may release one's tension and serve as a substitute for direct or indirect retaliation. Second, developing additional sources of emotional support (colleagues or family) may raise one's tolerance for the same level of manifest conflict. Third, decreasing one's future dependence upon the relationship reduces the costs of conflict without necessarily altering its form or resolving the underlying issues.

The way Mack and Sy each managed his end of the conflict at different points are illustrative. Mack coped with the threat posed to his career by stating his fear and inviting the reassurance he received from Dave, albeit not from Sy. Mack's overtures to Sy during the period between the consultant's visits were not reciprocated—and Mack felt rejected. He coped with these feelings in part by expressing them to Dave. Sy for his part was avoiding Mack in order to avoid the discomfort associated with dealing with him. Also, Mack continued to consider leaving the firm—one way of coping, not merely with his conflict with Sy, but also with his failure to receive the assignments he wanted.

Notwithstanding the appropriateness of the control tactics described here and in the section on preventing ignition of conflict, the overall strategy of conflict management could not be based on control alone in the Mack–Sy case. Certain considerations suggested that attempts to avoid or control the conflict alone would not be successful: there were too many reinforcing, self-perpetuating aspects of their conflict pattern, each with the further potential for actually escalating the conflict. For example, Mack's withholding assistance from Sy (which the latter resented), was undoubtedly related to the antagonism Sy communicated back to Mack.

Eliminate the Conflict Issues

The fourth operational objective of conflict management would be measured by the number and importance of the issues between the parties. The various strategies of control can have the effect of de-escalating the conflict to the extent of eliminating some of the symptomatic issues. However, eliminating the basic issues means resolving them, by reaching agreement where disagreement persists, achieving trust where distrust prevails, and so on. There is little to be said about this objective because it is the most obvious and straightforward, although it is often the most difficult to achieve.

Individual Initiatives and Direct Dialogue

The three types of control of conflict — avoidance, constraining its manifest form, and coping better with its consequences — can be pursued individually by each participant to a conflict. This may be better than no effort at all, but it seldom is as effective as it is when the parties jointly devise such control strategems. But coordinated forms of control require dialogue. So does, of course, the resolution of objectives.

6

Strategic Ingredients Supporting Productive Dialogue

The following ingredients in the interpersonal setting are postulated as strategic to productive dialogue.

1. Mutual positive motivation
2. Balance in the situation power of the two principals
3. Synchronization of their confrontation efforts
4. Appropriate pacing of the phases of a dialogue
5. Conditions favoring openness
6. Reliable communicative signs
7. Optimum tension in the situation

The discussion of each of these factors in the present chapter includes a proposition about the relevance of the factor to the success of a confrontation, a description of the underlying rationale or psychological mechanisms involved, and an analysis of those aspects of the three case studies which indicated opportunities for third-party influence.

Interpersonal Dialogue

Although differences in organizations may be handled exclusively by the strategies of avoidance, constraint, and improved coping methods, discussed in Chapter 5, there are potential advantages to a more direct approach to conflict management, which involves dialogue. Ideally, dialogue would lead to resolution, but failing that, to more constructive control strategies.

In dialogue, the parties directly engage each other and focus on the conflict between them. They explore the issues in conflict, the underlying needs or forces involved, and the feelings generated by the conflict itself.

If well managed, dialogue is a method for achieving greater understanding of the nature of the basic issues; for achieving common diagnostic understanding of the trigger tactics and consequences of their conflict; and for inventing control possibilities or possible resolutions.

In addition, when participants candidly express and accurately represent themselves to each other in a well-managed dialogue, they enhance the authenticity of their relationship and their sense of personal integrity. Even when there is no emotional reconciliation, if the parties devise better coping techniques, they feel more control over their interpersonal environment.

Candor does involve risks for participants. Openness about one's feelings in itself often violates organizational norms prescribing rationality and proscribing emotionality. Moreover, if one does not resolve the relationship issue, one's statements may serve to add further cause for the other's antagonisms. In any event, one may feel even more vulnerable because of what the other knows about him. Thus, an important task of conflict management includes maximizing the productivity of a dialogue and minimizing the risks involved.

Ensuring Mutual Motivation

Both parties must have incentives for resolving or controlling the interpersonal conflict. Without adequate incentive on both sides, there will be no give-and-take, in the sense either of emotional exchanges or substantive bargaining and problem solving. If one engages another to resolve a conflict and discovers that the second person was unaware of or indifferent to the conflict, this can be embarrassing. If the preliminary task for the initiating party turns out to be one of generating some incentive for the second to respond, the situation should be so defined as early as possible.

The third party can endeavor to learn each party's motivation, as well as the time frame within which each party views the adverse consequences of the conflict, prior to a confrontation initiative on either party's part. Important dissimilarities in motivation can lead to delaying or avoiding a confrontation, or it may influence the level of energy the more highly motivated party is encouraged to invest, the pacing of the dialogue, and expectations about incomes.

Let us review the motivational forces in the three case studies.

1. In the Bill–Lloyd case, Lloyd initiated a renegotiation of the intergroup relationship, but Bill had a compelling need to improve their interpersonal relationship. Lloyd's stated objections had established a bargaining point from which he could accede to more accommodating behavior if he were more satisfied with other terms of the relationship. Thus the important condition had developed that each was being inconvenienced by the other and both were aware of this interdependence. The third party played no role in certifying the mutual incentive to resolve their conflict. Bill had informed Lloyd of his intentions; the fact that Lloyd had readily accepted Bill's invitation to a meeting to work on their differences indicated that Lloyd had reciprocal interest.

2. Again, in the Fred–Charles case, both parties were troubled by the psychic costs of the conflict and the way their relationship interfered with their work. Both parties had independently sought the involvement of the consultant. Moreover, they received encouragement to work on their relationship from other members of the staff and the general manager. The above motivational conditions were all favorable. Only Charles's greater organizational insecurity made him somewhat more cautious in the confrontation.

3. The Mack–Sy case contained the most unfavorable motivational conditions initially, something not appreciated by the consultant prior to the confrontation. Sy's dependence on Mack was short run: he needed Mack's technical help and wanted to be able to demonstrate to his superiors (as well as to himself) that he was interpersonally competent and thereby qualified for

promotion. In contrast, Mack's dependence on Sy was primarily long term and conditional on Sy's promotion. Therefore, if Mack helped Sy look good, he improved Sy's chances of being promoted and becoming his boss. If he didn't help Sy and Sy was still promoted, he could never work for Sy. Therefore, Mack was motivated to maintain contacts with top-level people at headquarters and to begin looking for another job. Mack was not without some current motivation to resolve the conflict, but it was weaker than Sy's. The principals and Dave only became fully aware of the asymmetry during the confrontation when the consultant asked Mack whether he felt dependent upon Sy, and the answer was no. However, Mack's incentives for resolution were heightened by the conflict once it surfaced; he began to fear that continued conflict with Sy might be a major liability to his own career, whether or not Sy became his boss.

Achieving Balance in Situational Power

Power parity in a dialogue is most conducive to success. Perceptions of power inequality undermine trust, inhibit dialogue, and decrease the likelihood of a constructive outcome. Inequality tends to undermine trust on both ends of the unbalanced relationship.

How does it look from the point of view of the lesser power? Perhaps the most basic reason that another's power advantages undermine one's trust toward him is a general appreciation of the tendency for power to be used by those who possess it.

Why does a perceived power advantage undermine the stronger party's trust toward the weaker? The person with more power tends to interpret cooperative behavior by the weaker party as compliant, rather than volitional. This tendency derives from the peculiarities of causal attribution. Having power increases the tendency to assign a locus of cause to oneself. Without power, one can assign the locus of cause to the other.

Power imbalances also tend to inhibit the parties from advancing their respective views in a clear and forceful manner. The stronger party often feels, "Why should I have to elaborate my views?" Conversely, the weaker party can rationalize, "What's the use?" This reticence is significant because people usually are ready to modify their views on an issue only after they are satisfied that they have presented them effectively.

Situational power can be affected by various factors, including organizational status, political security, verbal skills, and the presence or absence of allies.

Therefore, the third party can attempt to avoid an overall imbalance by various means: by offsetting skill disadvantages via certain ground rules, by active interventions that ensure equal air time to less assertive participants, by helping a person who feels "one down" to make a point, or by including others who will provide relatively more support to the participant with less organizational power.

1. Regarding the Bill–Lloyd case, we have already confirmed that they both had adequate incentives to work on their conflict. Moreover, their situational power was in overall balance: Lloyd's aggressiveness, his somewhat greater taste for conflict, and his relatively greater ability to directly stress the other person in encounters were offset by the fact that Bill derived relatively more reassurance than Lloyd from the presence of the third party.

2. Some factors affecting the situational power in the Mack–Sy case favored Mack, others favored Sy. The analysis indicated Sy had a higher immediate motivation, which decreased his sense of potency and increased his frustration. However, Sy had the initiative during their first meeting. For this and other reasons, Mack felt "one down" in his encounter with Sy: Sy was the number-two man on the staff; Sy had teamed with his subordinate to confront Mack in a recent staff meeting; Sy had the longer consulting contact with Dave; Sy had more contact with the personnel manager.

3. Fred and Charles had symmetrical power in each of several respects. Both wanted to resolve the conflict. Both were skilled in holding their own in conflictful exchanges (albeit not necessarily in the techniques of conflict resolution). The third party was probably perceived as equally distant or close to both. The chief engineer who was present for part of their confrontation was chosen for his balanced positive relations with the two prin-

cipals. Charles's insecurity in the organization was one unbalancing factor; perhaps in an effort to offset this factor, Charles used several ploys designed to draw in the third party as an ally.

Synchronizing Confrontation Efforts

The initiatives to confront by one principal must be synchronized with the other's readiness for the dialogue, to avoid it being abortive. In practice, persons frequently have difficulty synchronizing their initiatives. One may choose a time and place not suitable to the other. If the second party later tries to confront in a different situation, the first, in the meantime, may have resolved to handle the differences by avoidance or indirect means, and the second party is now offended, further aggrieved, and more resistant to a dialogue.

Positive overtures in particular are likely to contribute more to conflict resolution when they are synchronized with the other's readiness to interpret them correctly and reciprocate.

Several psychological dynamics are involved here. The first is reciprocation: a person tends to reject someone who has appeared to reject him or her. The second is reinforcement: a person's tendency to make overtures decreases if his or her efforts do not receive positive responses. A third factor is involved because one's acts can usually be given more than one interpretation. A sincere effort to clarify the issues may be seen simply as an attack; or a conciliatory move can be interpreted as a sign of weakness, rather than as a positive overture from a position of strength.

1. Both Bill and Lloyd were prepared for their confrontation when it occurred, Bill having told Lloyd his reason for asking to meet. The third party's presence and limited availability helped synchronize their timing.

2. Similarly, in the Fred–Charles case, the consultant synchronized at various levels. The staff meeting discussion of how he should use his time allowed the parties to express in subtle ways any reluctance about confronting. This case, of the three studied here, contained decision-making processes that were most open to influence and required the greatest sharing of the initiative between the two principals. The third party also syn-

chronized moves during the dialogue. For example, he discouraged Charles from expressing high optimism about the prospects of an early resolution (a kind of positive overture from him) when Fred would quickly counter with a pessimistic prediction (which Charles then experienced as a rejection).

3. The Mack–Sy case provides an example of inadequate synchronization that we shall review in detail. Sy's relatively higher readiness was signaled by early clues that the third party should have attended to. The interpersonal conflict had first been exposed by Sy when he placed "the role of the controller" on the agenda. Also, Sy had named Mack in his preliminary interview with Dave, whereas Mack referred only to a conflict of some urgency. Following this pattern, it was Sy who invited Mack to the cocktail session and who initiated the dialogue at cocktails and the confrontation at the staff meeting.

Mack was less ready. His dependence on Sy was not as immediate as vice versa, he may have perceived a power disadvantage in the dialogue setting, and he may have felt some guilt and vulnerability for having withdrawn his assistance from the X Mill project.

Despite the asymmetry in readiness, the principals did meet. The overall decision to meet and work on the Mack–Sy conflict was an outcome of a series of choices in which the third party played a significant role. Let us review those choice points.

First, Dave counseled Mack that there was an optimum time lag after a person returns from a human relations training experience and undertakes heavy interpersonal work in an organizational context. If Mack accepted the notion, he would have been encouraged not to postpone his confrontation with Sy too long. In this early interview with Mack, however, Dave did not confirm that the idea made sense to Mack, nor did he determine whom Mack felt he "had to confront." Dave did not gain this information because he did not want to press Mack to identify his antagonist. Dave's stance was not particularly inappropriate at that time because he hadn't yet met with Sy. However, in view of later developments, it would have been valuable if Dave had taken special note of Mack's failure to name the other person involved, asking himself and perhaps Mack: Did the omission reflect a lack in Mack's trust or confidence regarding Dave or his uncertainty about the consultant's role? Confronting Mack with this question would have been potentially embarrassing; however, in view of the fact that Dave and Mack were discussing Mack's recent experiences in which interpersonal openness was normal, the risks were probably minimal.

Second, Dave chose to mention to Sy the possibility of a meeting of the three of them during his current visit. Sy immediately bought the idea and provided the initiative for following through. Dave was ambivalent, and asked himself several questions before agreeing to the meeting. For example, he asked, "Is Mack ready?" In fact, Mack had *not* indicated that he was ready for a dialogue with Sy. Dave relied upon inferences: Mack was currently wrestling with interpersonal issues; Mack had said he was determined to confront one member of the staff, whom Dave now assumed to be Sy. (Later this was confirmed.) The second question was more critical to Dave's decision to proceed: "Are Sy and Mack going to confront anyway?" Dave heard them both express a resolve to confront the other. Dave believed the prospects of a constructive outcome were higher with a third party like himself present. He also quickly decided that he could assume his personal responsibility for the meeting and the risks entailed, and that he had the energy to work that evening.

Third, Dave did not question or delay Sy's act to invite Mack, although he felt uneasy about it at the time. Sy's action had the advantage of being spontaneous, directly expressing his interest in getting together, and increasing his commitment. A disadvantage of Sy's quick move was that he and Dave did not have an opportunity to discuss what should be communicated to Mack about their expectations so that Mack's decision to join them would take these expectations into account. In inviting Mack to meet with himself and Dave, Sy apparently went no further than asking him to join them for drinks after work. Dave was uncomfortable in leaving it at this, but was more uncomfortable with the awkwardness of any existing alternative for contacting Mack before they met at the club. As a result neither Dave nor Sy ensured that Mack was aware of the agenda for the session. This denied him information that might have influenced his decision to accept the invitation and provided him with an opportunity to prepare himself mentally and emotionally. Dave only fully appreciated the degree of importance of this omission later in reviewing the entire episode.

Fourth, after they had been together for a brief period, the consultant indicated that his plans included the possibility of exploring and working on interpersonal relationships. Ordinarily, such a suggestion made to a group is not very coercive. It could be addressed or ignored. But in this case, three out of four already had this activity in mind. Clearly, Mack had less choice than Sy as to whether a dialogue would take place.

Dave's alternative at the outset of the meeting was first to share with Mack what had occurred in the afternoon and how it had been decided to meet; and then to allow Mack to react to the general idea of working on his relationship with Sy as well as to indicate whether this was the time and place.

To summarize the above discussion, the many decisions involved in arranging the first meeting and defining its purpose both reflected and contributed to the asymmetrical pattern of Sy's high readiness and Mack's low readiness for the dialogue. Ideally, the decision process would have had just the opposite effect, decreasing the asymmetry.

This asymmetry during Dave's first visit undoubtedly limited the progress that could be made in the first meetings and may have enhanced Mack's sense of the risks involved and his feelings that the dialogue had been rigged. For Sy's part, the resulting lack of engagement by Mack served to increase his frustration.

In the period between Dave's visits, the asymmetry was reversed. Sy became *less* available than Mack for further work on their relationship. Sy was busy during this period, but other factors were probably involved. Apparently, Sy's confidence in his own ability to confront Mack in a one-to-one setting and talk through differences was lower than Dave had assumed. A comment Sy made at the end of Dave's first visit reflected this idea, but it did not fully register with Dave until he was reviewing the entire episode. In any event, when Sy declined to respond to Mack's bids to engage in dialogue, the latter felt rejected and discouraged.

Finally, in preparation for the reconciliation meeting during his second visit, the consultant ascertained that both principals were motivated to work on their relationship and that the timing was right before he proposed the meeting to either one. During that meeting, he intervened to ensure that Sy responded verbally to Mack after the latter had made a self-disclosure and had begun to feel anxious about the meaning of Sy's silence.

Managing the Differentiation and Integration Phases

At least two phases of an effective conflict dialogue can be identified, a differentiation phase and an integration phase. The basic idea of the *differentiation phase* is that it usually takes some extended period of time for parties in conflict to describe the issues that divide them and to ventilate their feelings about each other. This differentiation phase requires that a person be allowed to state his or her views and receive some indication that these views are understood by the other principal.

In the *integration phase* the parties appreciate their similarities, acknowledge their common goals, own up to positive aspects of their ambivalences, express warmth and respect, or engage in other positive actions to manage their conflict.

A conflict-resolution episode does not necessarily include just one differentiation and one integration phase. It may comprise a series of these two phases; but the potential for integration at any point in time is no greater than the adequacy of the differentiation already achieved. To the extent that the parties try to cut short the differentiation phase, dialogues are likely to abort or to result in solutions that are unstable.

One requirement this imposes is that the third party be comfortable with both (1) a high level of sustained differentiation and the hostility and assertions of opposing goals that characterize the differentiation phase; and (2) the warmth and closeness often expressed as a part of the integration phase.

These two phases can be identified in all three cases. One case (Bill–Lloyd) illustrates the use of a third party for only one phase. The session in which Dave participated accomplished the differentiation. The only really integrative acts were to express confidence in their ability to continue the dialogue in general and to agree to a joint meeting of their groups in particular. The substance of the integrative phase was continued later.

The Mack–Sy case illustrates a differentiation phase involving two intensive sessions and one low-key session in which the conflict atmosphere had de-escalated. The interpersonally integrative session occurred many weeks later.

The Fred–Charles case perhaps best illustrates our view of these phases and also suggests some of the aspects of the dialogue format that correlate with these phases and can be influenced by a third party. The first phase of the Fred–Charles conflict occurred at the office and was confined to three persons. It involved clarification of divisive issues, identification of personal differences, review of past events, and escalation of ego-bruising behaviors. The second phase, at the restaurant and in an enlarged group, involved emphasis on common goals, identification of personal similarities between the principals, and a here-and-now orientation.

Stated in more general terms, the components of this sequence in the Fred–Charles case were as follows:

- Divisive, differentiating agenda followed by integrating topics
- Task issues followed by personal reactions
- "There-and-then" discussions giving way to more attention to the "here-and-now" process
- Simple social groupings gradually complicated by adding other persons (the preconfrontation phone interviews were followed by the three-person group, which was then enlarged to include another person)
- Work setting followed by more informal setting

Promoting Openness

Interpersonal dialogues frequently founder because the principals do not feel that they can be open with each other about their private opinions, perceptions, and feelings, which comprise the essential data for understanding their current conflict and finding a way to work out of it. Three factors significantly contribute to openness in the dialogue: relevant norms of the social system, the emotional reassurance available to the participants, and the "process skills" available for facilitating dialogue.

Many normative conditions supported openness in our three interpersonal relationships. All six principals previously had participated in a human relations workshop that emphasized the value of open expression of feelings and interpersonal dialogue. In the Bill–Lloyd case, these norms had become a part of the working process of the larger group. In both the Mack–Sy and Fred–Charles situations, their superiors and colleagues expressed support for the values of openness. In all three cases, the presence of a third-party consultant associated with human relations training further strengthened the normative support for openness and helped structure the setting for dialogue. Where such preconditions are not so favorable, separate sessions between the third party and the principals can provide the latter with practice in confronting, expression of feelings, and process analysis.

The presence of a third party, a consultant who can provide acceptance and emotional support, was reassuring to the participants in our cases. Reassurance is important because one of the reasons for not confronting an issue is that exposing an underlying issue in a conflict means owning up to resentments, rejections, and other feelings that the person himself does not like to admit. Many of us have been brought up to regard these feelings as "petty" and "silly" and as "being too sensitive." Also, as was stated in Chapter 5, one may believe that these feelings result from insecurities (about being competent or accepted) that one is unwilling to acknowledge, either to oneself or to someone else.

In all three cases, the skills possessed by the third-party consultant were perceived by the parties as decreasing the risk of an abortive dialogue. The third party also may have slightly increased the potential payoff from these dialogues in the sense that the participants believed that he could assist them in learning something of general value about their behavior in such situations.

Enhancing Communication

The dialogue will make no headway unless the principals each can understand what the other is saying. Even under conditions where one is striving to be open about intentions, opinions, feelings, and reactions to the other, various factors can limit the reliability with which the messages are read by the receiver.

A person responds to only some fraction of the available information. Persons utilize and interpret the available information in ways that tend to confirm, rather than disconfirm, their existing views. Two processes can contribute to this bias: selective perception and predisposed evaluation. Selective perception is the idea that a person perceives and utilizes information about which the person has little ambivalence, avoiding information that challenges attitudes which are not firmly held. Predisposed evaluation refers to the tendency to evaluate negatively, to discount, to refute information that one cannot avoid and that does not conform to one's existing attitudes.

If one is assumed to have done or said something one did not actually do, or if one is perceived as pursuing objectives one is not in fact seeking, a third party can perform a communication function increasing the validity of mutual perceptions. By skillful intervention, one party may come to better understand the other's position, especially the limited character of the other's demands and the integrity of the other's motive.

There are several benefits to correcting misperceptions that prompted or that fed a conflict. The person who achieves a more accurate perception can adjust to the reality. In addition, there is a possible psychological effect for the person who becomes better understood. When one finds that, despite efforts to explain oneself, one is not understood, the tendency is to feel frustrated with the situation, angry toward those who do not understand, and defensive. These feelings contribute to the conflict. If and when one finally is more correctly perceived, the person becomes more relaxed and feels somewhat more accepted just by virtue of being understood. As a result the person is more likely to critically review his own position and to modify it in ways that are responsive to the other person's views.

A third party can contribute to the general reliability of the communication by translating and articulating for the parties, by procedural devices, and by developing a common language for the dialogue. In addition, as we have already explored, synchronization contributes to the accuracy of the interpretation of signs.

In each of the three cases, Dave frequently would summarize what he had heard one person say and then check to see whether the person was satisfied with that statement. This reassured each person that he had adequately stated his position, or it provided an opportunity for him to make any corrections. Moreover, when the consultant was restating one person's views, the other person had another opportunity to understand the first's concerns. Understanding was promoted because the person was less likely to distort messages from a neutral, and because the consultant could crystallize the adversary's views. Finally, in restating a person's views, the consultant endeavored to characterize a party's position in a way that made it understandable and justifiable.

Dave would ask a person to repeat what he had just heard the other person say before he allowed the former to respond. A related procedure that is sometimes used with great success but was not employed in these three cases is "role reversal," where each person is asked to take the role of the other, to articulate and defend the other's position. Thus, the same dialogue between the principals is continued for a period of time with each playing the role of the other. Still another device sometimes used for similar purposes is tape recording the dialogue, which can be replayed by the participants in order to achieve greater understanding of what each was trying to say.

In each of the three case studies, both principals understood the technical terms being used and they shared important terms about the dialogue itself. For example, they used and understood the meaning of "feedback" and the distinction between one's "feelings" and one's "thoughts." Beyond that, the pairs of principals needed to develop a language for signaling priorities (the relative importance each person attached to the grievances he had with the other) and for making important distinctions (for example, to differentiate between the other's acts that challenge one's self-concept and those acts that make one's task work more difficult). It is not clear just how much language development actually occurred in each case or whether the third party played an instrumental role in this development.

Maintaining a Productive Level of Tension

The third party can influence the level of tension in the interpersonal system, which in turn affects the productivity of the dialogue. There is persuasive experimental evidence to support the idea that an individual's capacity for complex thinking is altered in a curvilinear fashion as stress increases, and that therefore, the individual's maximum ability to integrate and to utilize information occurs at some *moderate stress level.* The more specific effects of very high stress include consideration of fewer alternatives, rigidity, and repetition; reduction in the dimensionality of thinking (resulting in simpler perceptual systems); and reduction in the number of goals salient for the individual. High stress also increases tendencies to perceive threat and use power.

Observations of third-party consultation supports the relevance of the curvilinear model to interpersonal conflict:

1. If the threat level is low, there is no sense of urgency, no necessity to look for alternative ways of behaving, and no incentive for conciliatory overtures.
2. At a higher threat level, say moderate level, the person searches for and integrates more information, considers more alternatives, and experiences a higher sense of urgency in changing the situation.
3. At a very high level of threat the person's ability to process information and perceive alternatives decreases. This can produce rigidity of positions and polarization of adversaries.

Not only is the level of threat important, but the *direction of change* in the level of threat will combine with other factors to affect the productivity of dialogue at any point in time. For example, a brief period of high threat followed by a reduction of threat often leaves an after-image of the necessity for improvement and yet also currently provides a climate that allows for efficient information processing and exchange and behavioral change.

What factors influence stress? The concept of decontrolling the conflict is useful here. One way that conflict can be decontrolled and the tension level increased is merely by increasing the parties' exposure to each other. Increasing exposure can involve bringing them face to face, reducing the number of other persons present, limiting their avenues of escape from each other, and so on. A second way that tension can be increased is to instigate acts that sharpen the conflict issues between them (for example, shifting the focus of dialogue from a symptomatic to a basic issue, or citing the consequences of a failure to agree). A third means for increasing tension is promoting the exchange of perceptions. In emotional conflict, recognition of their mutual feelings is a step toward resolving the conflict but is stressful. These represent only a few illustrative factors that both influence the tension level and can in turn be influenced by the third party.

How did this function of tension management enter into the third-party role in our illustrative cases?

Throughout the Bill–Lloyd and Fred–Charles confrontations, Dave's interventions took into account the level of threat, stress, or tension. Encouraging them to share their negative perceptions and feelings certainly provided temporarily increased tension. He also used or encouraged humor to reduce the general level of tension or to make a specific piece of threatening information more acceptable.

In the Mack–Sy case, the tension level tended to be quite high from the start. The conflict was intensely felt. For Mack, an especially sharp increase in the threat level probably occurred when he learned the purpose of the first meeting and then when his failure to join the issue brought additional pressure from all the parties present.

Dave had two alternative strategies for encouraging Mack to join the issues: (1) add pressure on Mack to force him into the arena, or (2) provide support for him so that he would feel secure enough to participate. Upon reflection after the episode, Dave concluded that he probably should have provided Mack with more active support, and that he should have tried harder to see the situation as Mack was seeing it. The point is that even before Dave added his own pressure, Mack probably was above, rather than below, the optimum tension level for productive dialogue.

The case also presents material bearing on the longer-run effect of a temporary period of high stress. Sy's outburst at the staff meeting both reflected the very high level of stress he felt and produced a high level of stress in others in the staff group. The stress level was undoubtedly superoptimal in terms of immediate utilization of the data produced by the confrontation. Yet the third party did not attempt to terminate the confrontation or tactically to de-escalate it significantly. Several factors supported this choice, one of which was the assumption that the intense encounter and the after-images it created would lead to productive work subsequently. It did prove to be the climax that set the stage for the eventual improvements in the relationship.

The task of "tension management" after the intense confrontation changed somewhat in character. Tension needed to be reduced so that the parties could reflect upon and integrate the morning's experience. Tension reduction would be served if the principals, Mack and Sy, could gain at least indirect reassurance that other staff members did not disapprove of them as a result of the conflict, and if the other staff members could reassure themselves that the two adversaries were still intact after the morning confrontation. The fact that the staff group remained together and spent a prolonged lunch in rest and recuperation served these particular tension management needs.

Summary

If well handled, the direct dialogue between participants can result in resolution or better control of the conflict. The participants themselves or a third party can facilitate a productive confrontation by assessing and managing the following ingredients in the interaction setting: motivation, situational power, timing, pacing, tension level, communicative signs, and the group norms, process skills, and support relevant to openness.

7

Techniques for Managing a Dialogue

Having explored in Chapter 6 the ingredients conducive to productive dialogue, the analysis now focuses on preliminary interviewing, specific tactical choices to structuring the setting for dialogue, active facilitation of the dialogue meeting, and the planning for future work. Each of these can be influenced by the principals themselves and by a third party.

Preparing the Participants

Preliminary discussions between the potential third party and the individual participants are valuable. In the Fred–Charles case, conversations with each person in advance gave Dave information about issues, motivations, and readiness to work on the conflict. However, in the Mack–Sy case, Dave had less information than he needed, a point we have developed elsewhere. Similarly, in the Bill–Lloyd case, Dave chatted only briefly with Lloyd and did not learn his view of the conflict. One could argue the advantage of more preliminary work.

One-on-one discussions give the third party an opportunity to develop the norms and skills favorable to openness. By providing both challenge to and support for the clients, by furnishing the clients with feedback relevant to their immediate work, and by appropriate self-disclosures about his own uncertainties in the situation, the consultant can provide the clients with experiences that help prepare them for dialogue. Clients can quickly and successfully experience more openness than they would have expected, and develop confidence that openness can be managed in ways that will increase their effectiveness rather than their vulnerability.

Finding Neutral Turf

The site affects the balance of situational power. Neutrality was achieved in the Mack–Sy case, where the dialogue was initiated at the club, resumed at the staff meeting in the conference room, recapitulated at the club, and resumed at lunch during the consultant's second visit. As a contrast, the Bill–Lloyd dialogue occurred in Bill's large office. However, because the office was also frequently used for meetings even during Bill's absence, the territory was relatively neutral. The same point applies to the personnel manager's office where Fred and Charles held their initial dialogue. If it is desirable to offset a power advantage of one party, one can do this by deliberately favoring the other in the selection of the site.

Setting the Formality and Time Frame

The formality of the setting should fit the agenda. To illustrate, the Fred–Charles dialogue began in the office and then shifted to a much more casual setting, first a cocktail lounge and then a dining room. Although opposing considerations can be advanced, the following rationale supports the diversity and the sequence utilized in this case. In the office setting there is a greater sense of urgency to get on with whatever one is doing. This is helpful in identifying quickly many of the conflicting views and feelings. By shifting to the restaurant and by adding one round of drinks, the interaction could become somewhat more relaxed, allowing for a mixture of social banter and direct work on the relationship. This mixture facilitates the integrative and educative type of work that must follow the clarification of differences.

Another significant site choice was the director's decision to go to the club for lunch following the intensive confrontation between Mack and Sy. It was most conducive to rest, recuperation, and individual integration of the morning's experience.

The cases illustrate both inappropriate and appropriate time boundaries. For example, the time available for the meeting over cocktails turned out to be inadequate. It was especially unfortunate that Mack was the only one who was available to go on, inasmuch as it was he who had not prepared for the nature of the meeting in the first place. In retrospect, the course of the episode might have been quite different if Dave had been prepared to cancel his other meetings and had urged Sy to reconsider leaving at that point. In any event, Dave could have productively spent more time with Mack, especially given Mack's comment in the car that the session was cut short.

Open-endedness is especially important in the case of integrative and reconciliatory work. Thus, in the Mack–Sy case, it was just as important for the luncheon at the club to be open-ended as it was to be informal, in order for members individually and the group was a whole to assimilate the preceding events. Similarly, the reconciliation luncheon meeting between Mack and Sy was long and not time-bound — a fact essential to the work that was accomplished.

If both parties have a similar view of the time available for their interpersonal work, they are more likely to reciprocate each other's moves. For example, a person who assumes a short time period is more likely to make a premature conciliatory overture — a bid to shift to the integrative phase before they have thoroughly aired their differences.

Getting the Right Mix of People to the Meeting

The principals can work on their relationship by meeting alone, meeting with a third party, meeting with more than one third party, or meeting in the context of a larger group. Each additional person has many potential effects: he or she may add relevant perceptions and insights, may be perceived as a source of support, may increase the feelings of risk of one or both principals if not trusted or if he or she has power over one or both of their respective careers, may become identified as a third party for future work of the principals, and so on.

Several of these considerations are pertinent to the Fred–Charles case. The meeting started with the two principals and the consultant, but later the group was joined by the chief engineer. The consultant preferred to bring the issues to the surface in the smaller group. Recall that the earlier conflict incident related to the fifth-step grievance that occurred in the presence of several other persons. Fred had felt embarrassed about losing his objectivity. The effect of the audience on Charles had been different. The presence of his boss and the chief engineer had *added* to his incentive to be confronting. It had provided him with a "fringe benefit," namely, the opportunity to prove that he was willing to take risks. The consultant did not want Fred's participation in the dialogue, at least initially, to be inhibited or strictly objective. Rather, he wanted each to feel free to express his feelings, his subjective views. Similarly, the consultant did not want Charles to be stimulated to impress another member of the staff. Therefore, it would have been a mistake to have included additional persons in this first phase.

The addition of the chief engineer in the second phase added one more element of the larger organizational reality within which the two must ultimately work effectively. It had the potential of providing additional support and another source of perceptions, data from which the principals might derive insight.

In contrast with the above, the groupings for the Mack and Sy work were not always so appropriately composed. First, Dave chose to include the personnel manager as a fourth person in the *first* meeting. He wanted to help build an internal third-party role for this person, but he did not consult the principals. As it turned out, there were no advantages to including him.

The second encounter between Mack and Sy occurred in the staff group. The presence of others probably increased the perceived risks more than it added to the potential for either relevant data or support. While Dave could not have prevented Sy's outburst, he could have interrupted the interchange immediately after Sy's explanatory comments and suggested that the matter be pursued later in a smaller group. However, this intervention (which Dave did not even consider at the time) would have reduced the spontaneity of the interchange; it would have made everyone more, rather than less, anxious. Moreover, for better or for worse the matter was now a group as well as an interpersonal problem.

When the staff meeting broke for lunch after the intensive morning session, Dave actively sought to keep the group intact in order to allow members to provide each other with reassurances and to gradually reduce the general level of anxiety of members of the staff. In addition, as it turned out, it was useful to have all members of the staff present during the discussion initiated by Mack about Dave's role.

During his second visit, Dave limited the meeting to Mack and Sy. He didn't know what would happen but sensed the potential for constructive work. He later concluded that the presence of another person would have inhibited Mack's self-disclosures, which provided both the overture and the information that were the bases for reconciliation.

Refereeing the Interaction Process

The third party can regulate certain aspects of the process. For example, in the Fred–Charles case he terminated several discussions that had become either repetitive or counterproductive. He played an active role in generating shorter, more frequent interchanges. Rather than let a person go on at some length and introduce several ideas, he tried to allow each to respond immediately to a point already made by the other. He also sometimes sanctioned principals' behavior. As an example of a reward, Charles probably felt gratified when Fred (at Dave's inducement) differentiated Charles's "genuine regret" from his "false humility." During another interchange, Dave glowered at Charles, presumably to punish him for trying to use Dave's suggestion to his own advantage.

Initiating Agenda

The third party can play an active role in determining the agenda. As an illustration, the first interchange between Fred and Charles was focused on the task disagreement that had been identified in the staff meeting, a topic that did not require the third party to play an active role until he better understood how they related to each other. This and a second "agenda" item were clearly determined by the third party. Each was systematically pursued at some length. Later in the meeting, as the dialogue developed its own momentum, the focus of discussion shifted more rapidly and was influenced by all participants. The consultant's interjections — that is, his observations, reactions, and requests for others' reactions — became more frequent and continued to influence the focus of discussion, but often only to make a particular point.

Restating the Issue and the Principals' Views

A frequent third-party intervention is an attempt to summarize each party's views. Dave frequently made such a summary, and then checked to see whether the person agreed with his statement. As noted in the previous chapter, this helped the reliability of communication. In addition, these restatements sometimes helped terminate a discussion. Their summary quality not only gave closure to a particular discussion, but when the discussion had become a debate, it also sidestepped the question of who would have the last word.

Sometimes the third party's restatement redefined the issue in a more general form. For example, the question of whether management should make a tentative scheduling decision before or after Charles had contacted corporate personnel was translated into a jurisdictional issue. To have reached agreement on the specific decision, which happened to be of little practical import, would not have constituted progress in resolving the underlying differences.

Eliciting Reactions and Offering Observations

Another common third-party intervention is to encourage what is sometimes referred to as "feedback." For example, Fred and Charles exchanged their perceptions of each other, perceptions that governed their behavior toward each other. Dave also encouraged them to try to identify and understand the patterns in their current interactions and to share their current perceptions of, and emotional reactions to, each other.

The account of the Fred–Charles dialogue included instances where feedback may have yielded new insights. Fred appeared to gain insight into his tendency to be "feisty," to "lecture," and to bypass or exclude Charles. Charles gained a new appreciation of his own tendency to gloat when an adversary is being confronted by another person. The timing of such bits of feedback is important. Ideally they are given when they relate to some recent behavior and can also be heard by the principal involved.

Diagnosing the Conflict

The third party can focus the group's attention on diagnosis. The Mack–Sy case illustrates various types of interventions that generate or test diagnostic hunches.

First, during his session with Sy, Dave encouraged Sy to sharpen his insights into his own feelings toward Mack. Dave then tried to get Sy to identify the irritants he himself brought to the relationship. To sharpen the issue Dave described for Sy his own positive reaction to Mack.

Second, during the staff meeting encounter, Dave spelled out two alternative views of Mack's behavior: either as attempts to prove the mismatch between himself and his controller job, or as attempts to minimize the mismatch. If Mack were viewed as trying to highlight the mismatch, presumably this would be a self-defeating pattern in terms of Mack's career. Therefore, Dave believed Mack should know what impressions he was creating, and have an opportunity to reevaluate his own current behavior.

Third, during the rest and recuperation session, Dave offered his own assessment that Sy would not use this confrontation against Mack in the future, an assessment at variance with what Mack feared. It is not clear whether Mack was persuaded at the time.

Other aspects of the Mack–Sy conflict were not, but perhaps should have been, explicitly diagnosed, as, for example, the events in the staff meeting which had triggered Sy. As Chapter 5 emphasized, if the persons involved understand the triggering events, they can develop some relatively operational means for controlling the conflict in the future.

Prescribing Discussion Methods

The third party can prescribe discussion techniques to assist the parties in joining the issues. For example, during the first encounter in the Mack–Sy case, Dave asked Mack to show how his own personal problems related to his feelings about Sy. Such an inquiry often gives the person himself a new insight into the issues and the other person a way of responding. In this case, Mack declined, at least in part because he was not ready to confront Sy.

Dave took a similar action with Sy. Sy had just asked Mack to suggest the bases of his, Sy's, negative feelings. The third party noted that this was not a productive way to join the issue and urged Sy himself to provide the historical *data* about the events and incidents on which his feelings were based. Sy's subsequent statements became more helpful in clarifying his feelings.

In the discussion that followed, Dave allowed the principals to reveal many of the points of friction (without elaborating them), hoping there would be a dominant theme, and also wanting to see where the pair was headed. An alternative would have been to work on any one issue more thoroughly — for example, to try to get the principals to identify the practical differences involved.

Diagnosing Causes of Poor Dialogue

Often poor dialogue cannot be remedied by prescribing dialogue techniques. The third party must help identify more basic attitudes or other factors that are preventing productive dialogue. The Mack–Sy case provides illustrations.

In the first encounter, Dave identified and stressed the difficulty inherent in Mack's statement, "That is how I am." Mack communicated the attitude that there was no room for negotiation — either compromise or problem solving. It later occurred to Dave that he might have gone further and said to Mack, "Yes, that is how you feel right now as things stand. What condition would have to change, including those under Sy's control, that would allow you to feel differently?"

Throughout the first two encounters, Dave had gained a growing impression that the major difficulty in achieving any progress in the relationship was the imbalance between Sy's initiative in getting the issues out and Mack's reluctance either to join the issues or to show interest in improving the relationship. By identifying Sy's admitted dependence on Mack and Mack's denial of dependence on Sy, he underscored this as a roadblock, and subtly indicated that it might be wise to back off until Mack communicated direct dependence on Sy and thereby defined the situation more symmetrically.

Other Counseling Interventions

During discussion of strategic functions third parties perform, we noted several types of counsel that can be offered the principals: advising the appropriate timing for interpersonal dialogue; suggesting realistic expectations about the progress that can be achieved in the relationship; and urging colleagues of the principals to contribute in ways that are available to them.

A more direct form of counsel is illustrated by Dave's positive response to Mack's desire for techniques to change his relations with others. In contrast, he failed to counsel Sy in this way, despite the fact that Sy also expressed inadequacy in working on interpersonal issues. Dave had regarded Sy's behavior as adequate, and he himself was pressed for time; therefore, he didn't explore these feelings of Sy's. Given the fact that Sy subsequently avoided encounters with Mack, Dave missed an important cue here.

Planning for Future Dialogue

Generally the dialogue itself will increase the principals' capacity to continue to work on their relationship. A third party can take other steps to improve the effectiveness of continuing work by the two principals.

First, the general organization climate — apart from the immediate conflict — is important. Several elements of the climate of the organizations studied are relevant. For example, in the Mack–Sy case it was a norm for the staff to be open about its conflicts and it was legitimate to analyze group process. Staff members' interest in management development increased their willingness to confront a conflict because even if the relationship didn't improve, the experience could be developmental. In that sense there was less chance for complete "failure."

Second, the practice with dialogue techniques should have increased the principals' ability to use them, especially if these techniques or principles were made explicit by the consultant and stated in operations terms. It is possible for a third party to stimulate productive dialogue content and provide greater understanding about the conflict in question but not ensure that the principals themselves learn what ingredients made the dialogue constructive. For example, in the Fred–Charles case, the consultant merely terminated and derived some essential points from a discussion which had degenerated into an exchange of personal attacks. He missed an opportunity to lead a discussion of the destructiveness of that type of interchange and a diagnosis of how it was started and perpetuated. Such a group diagnosis might have resulted in the development of methods by which the principals could avoid ego-bruising interchanges in the future.

Third, the consultant can attempt to include another third party in the process, one who will be readily available to the principals. Involving the chief engineer in one case met this potential future need.

Fourth, it would have been helpful if Dave had been available to these three pairs over the next few weeks following the dialogue. This is especially relevant for the Mack–Sy case, considering Sy's inhibition about working alone with Mack on their relationship.

Fifth, the party can ensure that the principals have a specific time and purpose planned for getting together again. In the Bill–Lloyd case, an explicit decision was made by the parties to take some action steps; the third party received periodic reports and nothing more seemed to be required. If another meeting had been planned in the Mack–Sy case, Sy might have felt more choice between confronting Mack in the staff group in the morning or in the other session planned for later. Also, the principals had not agreed upon any plan for meeting again at the time the consultant departed, with the result that Mack's initiations were not reciprocated and no meetings occurred between the consultant's visits.

Summary

We have analyzed the many techniques and decisions that implement the functions set forth in the previous chapter. All of them can be performed by third parties; most of them by the principals themselves.

Many aspects of the setting for interpersonal work are both relevant to strategic ingredients of a dialogue and readily managed, including the neutrality of the site, the formality of the setting, the time frame for the meeting, and the composition of the group in which the dialogue occurs.

Innumerable possibilities exist for tactical actions relevant to the ongoing process: refereeing the interaction process, suggesting agenda, clarifying participants' messages, eliciting and offering interpersonal feedback, diagnosing the conflict issues, proposing discussion methods, diagnosing difficulties in the dialogue process, and counseling.

Planning for further dialogue will be facilitated when a third party attempts to teach the parties about the functions and techniques that have already facilitated or could potentially facilitate their dialogue. Ideally, some neutral person who has already been built into the process will be available for future third-party work if necessary. It is very important to ensure that the principals have agreed in specific terms to meet again.

8

Third-Party Attributes

What attributes does the third party need in order to perform the strategic functions and implement the tactical interventions to resolve conflicts? What problems are frequently encountered in establishing the appropriate role? What is the potential for organizational peers, superiors, and staff personnel to perform useful third-party functions?

Professional Expertise and Personal Qualities

The professional and personal qualities attributed to the third party that facilitate dialogue include diagnostic and behavioral skills, attitudes of acceptance, and a personal capacity to provide emotional support.

Professional identity with human relations training makes it easier for a consultant to be perceived as someone able to promote interpersonal dialogue. Demonstrated consulting skill in previous projects within the same organization also lends confidence in the consultant's ability.

In other situations, establishing the appropriate role identity and personal attributes may be a significant part of the third party's total job in assisting two parties in conflict. Private discussions with each principal may be used as a basis for judging the likelihood that the third party can make a positive contribution.

Appropriate Power and Knowledge

The perceived power of the third party and the general knowledge of the principals and issues are important attributes. It is an advantage for the third party to have little power over the futures of the principals in order to decrease the participants' sense of risk in confronting issues candidly and tendency to seek the approval of the third party. In the three cases studied, the third party had no such power, but in each case he had a close relationship with the principals' superior. Therefore, despite the consultant's efforts to preserve a nonevaluative stance toward organizational members and to preserve the confidentiality of all his separate relationships, it seems reasonable to believe that participants perceived some potential advantage in presenting their preferred image to the consultant. This issue was sharpened for the consultant when he later discovered that Charles's termination was linked in the minds of some organizational members with the conflict between Charles and Fred.

The third party does need another type of power: influence over the choice of setting, composition of group, agenda, and phasing. At least moderate knowledge of the principals, issues, and background factors usually is an advantage. It enhances the third party's credibility with the principals, increases the likelihood that his or her interventions will be on target, and reduces the amount of time that the principals spend talking to the third party rather than each other. However, if the third party is *highly* knowledgeable about the situation, it is harder to believe that he or she does not have opinions about the issues or the individuals.

Neutrality

Differences in the third party's relationships can influence his effectiveness. First, it is usually important for a third-party consultant to be neutral regarding the substantive positions of the parties and the outcome. This could have become an issue in the Bill–Lloyd case because of Dave's prior association with an issue in the conflict; Dave had participated in the team-building session that created the open, fluid pattern of group functioning that Bill wanted to preserve and Lloyd said he wanted to change.

Second, it is usually best for the third party to be comparably related to the principals in a personal sense. Only the Fred–Charles case illustrates this ideal. The consultant's short-term relationships with both persons were friendly, but professional. Dave had information about the parties and also some assurance of the esteem in which he was held and the type of consultant-role identity they attributed to him. Both Fred and Charles had mentioned the possibility of gaining Dave's active third-party assistance during his next visit.

The third party was closer to Bill at the outset of his dialogue with Lloyd. Dave's prior consulting with Bill made it impossible for him to quickly become similarly related to Lloyd — in terms of personal respect and trust. Nevertheless, Dave probably should have found a way to spend more time with Lloyd before the confrontation. As it happened, this initial asymmetry did not interfere, apparently because Lloyd attached more importance to Dave's professional identity than to his personal relations. Later, Lloyd said:

> Yes, I recognized that Dave was closer to Bill and the group, but I didn't assume he was therefore biased. This gets into professionalism. I assume that Dave, in his professional role, has his own built-in gyros keeping him neutral. Sure he confronted me about some of my behavior and made me uncomfortable, but he couldn't be a dish rag and still be effective, either.

The Bill–Lloyd case illustrated a third issue of neutrality — namely how the third party's approach can favor one of the principals. The norms of openness, acceptance, emotional support, and analysis of group process that the consultant brought to the dialogue were those Bill favored. Considering Lloyd's relative concern about excessive "groupiness" in the larger task group, one might have expected him to either resent or resist the consultant's methodology. As it turned out, he participated fully, utilizing the process to get his own views and concerns out in a forceful way. Moreover, the process was general enough to allow him to utilize bargaining behavior (for example, to hint at contingent actions if the two of them could not reach agreement). Thus, the potential disadvantage to Lloyd did not materialize.

The tactical asymmetries that occurred in the Mack–Sy case did have adverse consequences. Dave's earlier actions allowed Sy to participate in the decision to meet with Mack but did not even ensure that Mack was informed of the purpose of the meeting. Clearly, for reasons we have analyzed in detail in earlier chapters, this placed Mack at a disadvantage and led to his feelings that the confrontation had been "rigged."

If basic trust in the third party is high, it is less costly for him to give more support to one party's ideas, perceptions, feelings, and actions. In fact, where the consultant has a much better relationship with one party, he is better able to confront that party forcefully and introduce content threatening to that party. He also is better able to make interventions that interrupt, interfere with that person's present approach, or place restrictive ground rules on that person (such as "keep quiet and listen" or "would you try to state what you heard him say").

Work on the Role Relationship

The attributes described emphasize the more given aspects of a third party's role relationship to the conflict principals. The dynamic aspects are illustrated by the deterioration that occurred in Dave's relationship with one principal in the Mack–Sy case.

After the second meeting Dave learned Mack's perceptions that the first meeting had been "rigged" and his trust toward Dave damaged. It now becomes clear that Dave had missed an earlier opportunity to encourage Mack to raise such an issue when Mack drove Dave back to the motel after cocktails.

The circumstances under which Mack finally did state his feelings about Dave are significant. It followed Dave's expression of his own irritation with another person, the personnel manager. By expressing personal negative feelings, he became more available as a target, rather than wholly protected by his professional role.

Mack's perceptions concerned Dave. He wanted to be understood: if Dave had not maintained Mack's confidence it was through an omission in judgment. Dave's efforts to repair his relationship with Mack included the following: Dave explained the steps involved in the decision and objected to the interpretation "rigged"; he humorously claimed his good intentions; he emphasized the importance of trust to him in his role; and later, in touching base with Mack before departing, he expressed the positive concern he had for Mack.

Evidently, after Mack's expression of his feelings to Dave and the dialogue that ensued with Dave, his feelings toward Dave changed. His phone calls to Dave reflected growing trust and confidence. Finally, the visit during which the reconciliation occurred confirmed that they had developed a close, trusting relationship.

Internal Consultants: Organizational Peers and Superiors as Third Parties

An outside consultant may sometimes be in the best overall position to operate effectively as a third party. Nevertheless, organizational members potentially can play important third-party roles. Figure 8–1 depicts the several types of organizational role relationships considered here.

On the basis of the discussion earlier in this chapter, we propose five role attributes for identifying potential third parties from within an organization and for judging the potential effectiveness of persons who would be third parties:

1. High professional expertise regarding social processes
2. Low power over the fate of principals
3. High control over confrontation setting and processes
4. Moderate knowledge about the principals, issues, and background factors
5. Neutrality or balance with respect to substantive outcome, personal relationships, and conflict-resolution methodology

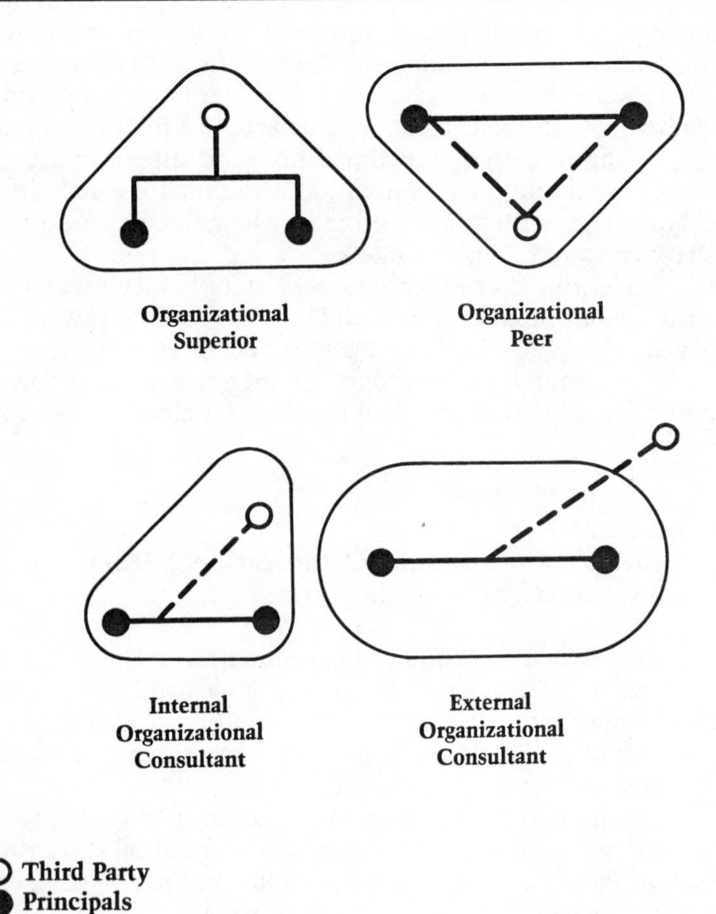

Figure 8–1
Organizational Relationships Between Third Parties and Principals

Many large organizations provide organizational consulting as a service supplied by the personnel department or some separate staff unit. How well do internal organizational consultants usually match these requisite role attributes? They frequently are seen as possessing sufficient professional expertise, although not as much as is attributed to the outside consultant. This edge in expertise held by the external consultant may be offset by the advantage of the internal consultant's more continuous availability. Internal consultants are more likely than outside consultants to be regarded as having an optimum amount of background knowledge. They usually can acquire sufficient control over the setting and process. However, the internal consultants encounter slightly more difficulty than external ones in demonstrating low power over the future of the principals and in achieving perceived neutrality.

Organizational peers who have an interest in, but no formal responsibility for, performing third-party functions are at a somewhat greater disadvantage than are internal consultants. Typically, it is more difficult for them to establish the requisite professional expertise and neutrality and to gain sufficient control over the setting and process. Moreover, they are often perceived as having superoptimal knowledge about the principals, issues, and background factors.

Organizational superiors are operating under the greatest handicap, even if they are perceived as having high professional expertise and do have high control over process. They tend to have high power over the careers of subordinates and it may be difficult for them to establish neutrality.

The tendencies just described are general. One would expect to find considerable variation among persons within each class of organizational role as well as among outside consultants.

Being Oneself

I have attempted to develop a general third-party theory and to outline generally applicable third-party practices. It must be acknowledged that the acceptance of "Dave" as a third party and the impact of his third-party interventions were conditioned by various personal attributes and patterns. He manifested a predilection for confrontation in his own encounters with others; he had a high energy level that sometimes had the effect of energizing the process; his changeable moods from extreme patience to impatience and abruptness were sometimes consistent and sometimes inconsistent with the needs of the situation; he had a high need to achieve an analytical understanding of what was happening, which was combined with a tendency to be emotionally moved with concern and empathy for a person struggling to express himself, to articulate his feelings, and to engage another; he occasionally was anxious about whether the dialogue would help or hurt the relationship, and whether or not his interventions would facilitate it, and so on.

Although it is *not* important for the general theory or general practice to incorporate these aspects of Dave's personal style or the way he comes across to others, these factors probably would have to be taken into account if one were to more fully understand what happened in these three or any other specific cases. Moreover, it *is* important for the general theory and practice to know that such personal attributes and styles do condition the role and the interventions of the person; his or her personal attributes must fit what he or she is trying to do in a third-party (or in any other) facilitative role.

9

Extension of the Dialogue Concept—to Intergroup Conflicts

The approach to dialogue and third-party consultation first developed in and for organizational contexts can be adapted to intergroup conflicts. I have adapted the concepts and methods to a number of intergroup settings, including labor–management relations on several occasions and informal international problem solving on one occasion. I report on the international application here in part because it is the only one of these experiences that has been thoroughly documented. Moreover, for a number of reasons it required more adaptation of the dialogue approach than did the applications to labor–management relations. Therefore, in a sense the case example presented below and the cases analyzed earlier "bracket" the labor–management applications. I will return to that point after presenting the international example, when I attempt to derive its general implications for dialogue in intergroup settings.

A Workshop Dialogue on Border Disputes in Africa

Against a history of border wars and bloody clashes between Kenya and Somalia and Ethiopia and Somalia, six participants from each of these countries met on neutral turf and participated in a two-week workshop to search for solutions to their border disputes.[1] I was among a team of Americans who facilitated their dialogue workshop in August 1969.

The clashes between the Somalis and their neighbors involved ambushes, plunder, and poisoned wells in the disputed territories. These clashes had many of the episodic characteristics of conflict described in Chapter 5, including similar proliferation tendencies and an evolving mixture of emotional and substantive issues. Emotions between countrymen of these countries, especially those who lived or grazed their cattle across the disputed territories, ran deep and raw.

Unlike the interpersonal dialogues analyzed earlier in this volume, the participants were not themselves the principals to the basic dispute in that they were not official representatives of their respective governments. Therefore, they could not themselves take direct steps to control or resolve the conflict.

The dialogue in this setting had a more limited (but still ambitious) objective. The overall purpose of the workshop was to bring together members of the elite of the three countries to analyze the conflict issues and the primary concerns of each country and to generate a promising avenue for solutions that could then become the subject of formal diplomatic discussion between their governments.

The operational task of managing the dialogue was to develop working relationships among the participants to permit them to engage in creative problem-solving processes.[2] The American third-party group never had any illusions that this would be easy. The geopolitical tensions among the countries in

---

[1]This account is based on an article previously published by the author. Reprinted by permission of *J. Appl. Beh. Sci.*, 6, 4:453–489. "A Problem-Solving Workshop on Border Disputes in Eastern Africa." © 1970 NTL Inst.

[2]The workshop described in Chapter 9 is one of about a half dozen problem-solving workshops documented in the literature which relate to intense and violent conflict between countries or communities. (J. Burton, 1969; L. Doob, 1970, 1973, 1976; B. Hill, 1982; H. Kelman, 1979; R. Walton, 1970.) Some of these workshops have had as major objectives to conduct research on conflict and to teach participants how to deal with conflict. In contrast, the dialogue workshop developed here is primarily focused on contributing to the better management of the conflict in question. Any research or education objectives would be pursued as a means to the specific conflict management objective or as a secondary objective.

conflict, the negative stereotypes that characterized their countrymen's perceptions of each other, and the highly emotional nature of the recent clashes made it a difficult challenge to develop the mutual respect, mutual trust, and the quality of communication required to engage in the conciliatory and creative problem-solving processes we sought.

The primary dispute between Somalia and Ethiopia involved the areas of the Ogaden and the Haud, areas within the de facto borders of Ethiopia but largely inhabited by Somali tribes. The dispute between Somalia and Kenya involved a district in northeastern Kenya that is heavily populated by people of the Somali culture.

The Somali constitution stated the goal of "Greater Somalia," which would unite the ethnic Somalis living in the adjacent areas of Ethiopia, Kenya, and French Somaliland. The Somali state itself was born in 1960 in an act of fusion between the ex-British and ex-Italian Somalilands, thereby providing a historical achievement that serves to bolster the Somalis' aspirations for the larger union.

The decade after the birth of the Somali Republic was marked by innumerable border incidents, each incident involving the killing of small numbers of men and as a whole promoting heavy military expenditures by the countries. Twice during this period the tensions in the border areas erupted into war, first in the Ogaden of Ethiopia in 1963 and then in northeast Kenya in 1966–67. During the mid-1960s Somalia began to accept large-scale arms assistance from the Soviet Union, complicating the military political situation in the Horn of Africa because Kenya received military aid from the British and Ethiopia from the United States.

During 1967–69 détente policies characterized relations between Somalia and each of its two neighbors. The governments issued joint statements intended to normalize relations, including agreements to exchange ambassadors, lift trade embargoes, and resume direct air service between capitals, and refrain from subversive activities against each other. Both the Communist and Western powers welcomed the détente initiatives of the Somali Republic. However, no sooner would a new joint communiqué be issued than new border incidents would disturb relations, especially with Ethiopia. For example, just weeks before the workshop, two serious incidents occurred, reminding Somali politicians of their commitment to irredentism. The incidents, in which about 50 persons were killed and 100 wounded, resulted from Ethiopian officials' efforts to collect a head tax on the livestock of Somali tribesmen in the Ogaden.

None of the steps to relax tension touched the basic issues in dispute. Somalis believed that the Somali-speaking people and the lands they inhabit should be united. In addition to moral and sociologically based arguments, the Somalis contested the 1897 treaty between Britain and Ethiopia, upon which Ethiopia based its definition of the northern border with the Somali Republic. They also cited an impartial investigation by the British in 1962 which showed that five of six residents in Kenya's northeastern district wished to leave Kenya to become part of Somalia. For their part, Ethiopians asserted legal and historical rights to the disputed areas in the Ogaden and the Haud. Both Kenya and Ethiopia invoked the principle of respect for the sovereignty and territorial integrity of states. They did not want to give up any territory, not only because of the value of the territory itself but also because to cede territory to Somalia's claims would make the multinational, multilingual states of Ethiopia and Kenya more vulnerable to other claims or secessionist movements.

The initiator of the workshop was Leonard Doob, professor of psychology at Yale University, who had developed an interest in this part of Africa. He enlisted two Yale colleagues, a lawyer interested in legal aspects of an economic community in East Africa and a political scientist interested in the federation in Africa. They developed the concept in 1966 but had difficulty raising funds and in securing the cooperation of all three governments. For example, in 1967 the Ethiopian government declined, and in 1968 the Somali government withdrew its consent. Finally, in 1969, all three governments agreed and funds were secured.

The participants from Ethiopia and Kenya were drawn from universities. The participants from Somalia, which does not have a major university, included a member of the opposition in Parliament, an educator, an editor, and high-level officials in the Institute of Public Administration, the Ministry of Education, and the Ministry of Planning. The three Yale organizers invited onto their team four third-party consultants who brought expertise in diplomacy, group dynamics, and third-party interventions. The staff of consultants and organizers met in Rome on August 1. The planning of the workshop design was conducted under poor circumstances: none of the consultants had met the Yale organizers; all were fatigued from the overnight transatlantic flight; and they were pressed for time. The lack of planning time resulted from scheduling difficulties.

They readily reached unanimous decisions regarding the first three of the following major areas of design:

1. *Phasing:* In Phase 1 the emphasis would be on developing communication relationships and promoting receptivity toward and skill in the diagnosis of group process—conditions that we assumed would promote more effective treatment of the border issue. Phase 2 would emphasize the search for viable solutions to the dispute.

2. *Activities:* A mixture of techniques would be used to facilitate the work, including simulations, theory seminars, and critiques of meetings.

3. *Schedule:* The typical work schedule would involve two morning sessions, an early afternoon session, an afternoon break followed by a social hour, and an evening session. A two-day break would occur in the middle of the workshop.

4. *Groupings:* This issue was not so easily resolved. All four consultants believed that the community should be divided into two working groups comprised of one half of the contingent from each country. However, differences centered on whether they should become the dominant grouping from the beginning. Three consultants believed they should. One urged a design that began with participants meeting initially in national groups. The majority view prevailed.

5. *Operational goal:* The Yale organizers stated that a goal for the two weeks was to achieve a consensus for some proposal to solve the border dispute. It was presumed that the proposal would be committed to writing but undecided whether it would be released to the press at the end of the conference or treated confidentially by individual participants.

Phase 1 of the Workshop

The three national groups arrived in Rome, and they and the American team boarded a chartered bus to the Hotel Fermeda in a small mountain town in northern Italy. The fourteen-hour overnight bus trip was numbing. The Somalis sat together, the Ethiopians were more dispersed, and the Kenyans most dispersed. (This clue to cohesion within teams foreshadowed the workshop's social structure.)

Orientation and Grouping

On Saturday evening and Sunday the participants were introduced to the methods of the workshop and to one another. After a general session on Saturday evening the participants were assigned to two working groups. (See Table 9–1.) This account draws heavily on the experience of Working Group II, usually referred to here as simply the "group." (The experience of Group I generally can be assumed to be similar, unless a contrast is specifically drawn.)

These working groups were intentionally unstructured in two important respects. First, the consultants who announced the group assignments and scheduled time for them did not specify

Table 9–1
Makeup of Working Groups

	Working Group I			Working Group II		
Somali participants	S_1	S_2	S_3	S_4	S_5	S_6
Kenyan participants	K_1	K_2	K_3	K_4	K_5	K_6
Ethiopian participants	E_1	E_2	E_3	E_4	E_5	E_6
American organizers		O_1	O_2		O_3	
American consultants = Planning Committee		C_1	C_2	C_3	C_4	

any substantive agenda or any mechanism for deciding upon such an agenda. Second, the consultants did not provide for any chairmanship for discussions. Instead they stressed that the time allotted could be used in any way each group chose; but group members were urged periodically to discuss their individual reactions and assessments of the group process to sharpen their skills in diagnosing process and to improve group functioning. The consultants provided illustrations of process analysis and authentic communication and rapport among members.

Participants responded to the emphasis on "process" with a mixture of acceptance and resistance. The inevitable floundering occurred as members endeavored to evolve some modus operandi. Members rejected each other's influence and canceled each other's initiatives. Frustration in the group mounted. Finally, on Sunday night, a climax of frustration precipitated the group's first planning decision. Members agreed to form a committee to select a topic of discussion for the next group meeting on Monday.

Legitimating Individual Differences

The Monday afternoon session illustrates the development of increasing capacity for coherent discussion and respect for individual differences. The topic was the role of the Organization for African Unity (OAU).

This discussion was more disciplined than preceding ones. One speaker from each country was heard from before a second person from the same country spoke. This occurred by tacit understanding. Eventually every member participated. In fact, although the formally allotted time had run out, there was general insistence that the last man have his say.

Significantly, the difference in views on the OAU did not follow country lines. Thus, the discussion reflected and reinforced growing individuation among Group II members. For example, K_4 outlined a pragmatic position that the OAU does not have effective power in such disputes, and that the only hope to end the border dispute in the Horn depends upon the parties' calculating the costs and coming to terms. E_5 disagreed in principle, reflecting somewhat more optimism about the role of the OAU. Still his faith in the OAU was more qualified than that of his countryman, E_6. Dissenting sharply from the views of both E_5 and E_6, E_4 deplored the corruption of existing institutions such as the OAU and stressed the need for revolutionary solutions. K_5 took a position closely related to E_4. S_5 dismissed the OAU on grounds of ineffectuality.

Many individuals "telegraphed" philosophies and interpersonal styles that would govern their approach to future discussions of the border disputes. For example, agitation developed between E_5 and K_4, but it appeared to be as much stimulated by interpersonal rivalries as by substantive disagreement. Both persons were intellectually keen; both spoke in paragraphs rather than sentences, developing several points each time they participated. Their similarities in style fostered competition for "air time" and for intellectual primacy.

Stock-taking: Satisfaction with Process and Progress

Late Monday afternoon the community paused to review the past twenty-four hours and assess progress. Several subgroups met to discuss their reactions and then presented a brief report to the general assembly. Participants were positive about the simulation and the afternoon discussion. The earlier frustration was being replaced by a sense of progress and optimism. The organizers read a telegram they had just received from the United Nations expressing encouragement for this experiment in informal diplomacy.

Discussion of Secondary Topics and Improvement in Group Functioning

Monday evening to Wednesday morning was a period of consolidation and preparation, building toward a confrontation of the border issues. The content of the discussions was related to but not directly focused on the dispute. Participants learned about the politics and cultures of the other two countries. For example, they explored the degrees of concentration of power in each country and its causes and consequences. Interpersonal relationships were being strengthened and the group was developing a more effective modus operandi.

The group was learning how to exploit the potential of low structure. Participants became flexible in managing the agenda and in adapting the group's structure. For example, when it was decided to engage in some systematic education about the internal problems faced by each country, the group decided to caucus briefly by country trios, and then organized to do the job efficiently.

The group became more effective in handling differences. Differences were carefully clarified, and persons sometimes changed their positions on the basis of different factual assumptions offered by other participants. When differences were not easily resolved, there was neither pressure to smooth over them nor any emotional outbreak.

Participants became more relaxed with one another. For example, on Tuesday evening the group began in a joking mood. E_4 entered the room and moved toward the couch, where three persons were already seated, indicating by his actions that he wanted to sit on the far end. This would have required S_5 to move over toward the center of the couch. Thus S_5 and E_4, who had been verbal combatants on many previous occasions, were now in a face-off over who would occupy a space they both preferred. For a while S_5 made no effort to move in either direction to make room for E_4, and when he finally did move it was toward the end of the couch, thereby denying E_4 the place he had tried to claim. Both had enjoyed the sparring match. Other group members also engaged in horseplay, frequently with a fraternal overtone that combined friendliness and rivalry.

Trust-building initiatives were reciprocated. In one instance, tears came to the eyes of a person as he described his doubts and fears about the capacity of his government to meet the great needs of his people for economic development. Others quietly urged him and his fellow countrymen to continue. Later other participants described weaknesses of their own countries. There was no disposition within the group to exploit revealed cracks in the national images. The mood was one of respect and understanding.

One brief interchange illustrates the attempts by participants to improve their patterns of communicating. K_4, who was prone to make very lengthy contributions to an ongoing discussion, had just finished one such dissertation. S_4 asked K_4 a simple, clarifying question to which K_4 could have provided a one-syllable answer. Again K_4 gave a lengthy reply. When he finished, E_4 said to K_4, quietly but pointedly, "Your answer was *Yes*?" K_4 replied "Yes" and fully appreciated the point.

Frequently during or at the conclusion of a session, one of the process consultants would initiate a critique of the way the group was functioning, which would lead to some interpersonal feedback or diagnostic insight into group process — for example, how the topical theme of the discussion had some relevance to dynamics of the group and vice versa.

Simulation and Theory Inputs

On each of the first three days a simulation exercise lasting from 1½ to 4 hours was used to illustrate conflict management concepts. Two simulations confronted participants with choices of either competing or cooperating with other players in striving toward their goals. These experiences allowed the workshop community to explore ideas such as interdependency, reciprocity, perceptions, expectations — to mention a few. They were intended to improve the processes of managing conflict and build collaboration within the two workgroups, and to provide diagnostic concepts relevant to the border disputes. Because these simulations involved subgroups composed of an Ethiopian, Somali, Kenyan, and American, they also accelerated the formation of interpersonal bonds across national groups.

Transfer of Control to a Planning Committee

Wednesday morning until Thursday afternoon was a period of transition to Phase 2. Late on Wednesday morning the consultants announced a procedure for achieving a relatively complete and efficient preliminary airing of the issues. Participants were to meet that afternoon as national groups and prepare statements of the issues to be presented in a general session the following morning. Meetings of Working Groups I and II were scheduled for Wednesday evening.

All three national groups met during the afternoon, although the Kenyans and Ethiopians met only briefly. There seemed to be some avoidance behavior (clustering in social activities and procrastination on the task), indicating negative feelings about the task or tension within the national groups. When the groups met that evening, the staff learned that the Somalis had not finished the tasks and that some Somalis preferred to continue working on the task as national groups rather than meet as working groups.

Before adjourning the evening session, the participants discussed their feelings about the task that the consultants had designed. First, one Kenyan objected to forming national groups, explaining, "After all, the idea is that we are individuals, speaking for ourselves, not our countries." There was only mild support for this view, and it came from other Kenyans. Second, an Ethiopian objected to the format of the presentation. He was supported by a second Ethiopian and a Kenyan. A third complaint was that participants should have been consulted in planning the task. This dissent received general support. Later that night the staff worked out a mechanism for transferring power to the total community.

During the first five days the consultants had decided how to allocate time to activities. They had sought evaluative reactions to each element of the design and considered these reactions; nevertheless they had preserved the initiative in design decisions. Now a representative committee would assume the authority and responsibility heretofore exercised by the four consultants.

The idea of broadening responsibility for the planning was accepted by the total workshop comunity Thursday afternoon. The representative planning committee was balanced both by working group and by national affiliation. These representatives were named in meetings of the national groups. Two consultants and one Yale organizer were on the committee.

The planning committee appeared to have immediate legitimacy and functioned effectively as a unit. It opted to have a permanent chairman for the committee itself; but it decided to have the Assembly (general assembly of the community) chaired by participants not on the committee, generally changing the chairmanship for each session by rotating the position among Somalis, Ethiopians, and Kenyans.

Phase 2 of the Workshop

Broaching the Conflict Issues

Let us return to the tasks that the consultants had assigned to the national groups on Wednesday morning:

Tasks for National Groups

Task I

As individual [Somalis, Kenyans, Ethiopians] list on newsprint (large sheets of paper) key grievances or disputes your people have with each of the other countries.

Task II

On a second sheet of newsprint list your predictions of the grievances or disputes that the individuals from each of the other two countries will bring regarding your country.

Be prepared to bring these written lists for Task I and Task II to a diagnostic general meeting in the main session room at 9:00 Thursday morning, with a representative prepared to explain your lists.

The tasks were intended to use a consistent format for identifying the issues and their symptoms. Beyond identifying points of friction from one's own view, the approach was intended to induce each national group to attempt to "take the role of the other" and to anticipate how one's own country was viewed by the people of the two other countries.

On Thursday morning the Somalis led off with their presentation, followed by Ethiopians, then Kenyans, and finally the Yale group, who had tried to predict the "grievances" that would be identified by each national group. The Somalis followed the format and attempted to predict the others' views toward Somalia. They were quite facile in articulating the views of others. Rejecting the suggested format, the Ethiopians presented a single listing of the issues. The Somalis objected because the list never mentioned the Somali Republic and aroused suspicions that the Ethiopians might be laying some historical claim to the whole of the Horn. The Kenyans likewise presented only one view of the dispute, a view that the Somalis believed was clearly biased. Reflecting on the presentations, one Somali said:

> I was disappointed that the Ethiopians and Kenyans did not follow the approach as we did. We are a free people. You can see that from how we presented both views. We appointed a lawyer for Ethiopia and for Kenya. We not only could see it from their view, but also we were free to *express* it from their view. But Ethiopians could not present our views. Nor could the Kenyans. This illustrates an important difference. In our land, two men may go to court — at great expense — because one claims a camel in the possession of the second. Then if the first is awarded the camel, he may allow the second to keep it. Why? Because it was an exercise for them. We can view disagreements in this way.

Interestingly, this Somali was able to view the morning's presentation as a product of cultural differences rather than seeing it strictly as a tactical exercise.

Abortive Effort to Join the Issues in the Assembly

In its initial meeting on Thursday afternoon the planning committee had decided that future work on the border issues would generally occur in the Assembly. The committee had developed an agenda for subsequent discussion, which is presented below.

I. A. What is a nation? What is a national state? What is the principle of self-determination?
   B. What is the nature of the problem?
   C. What are the implications of redrawing the map of northeast Africa?
II. How do these disputes hinder internal development and regional development?
III. External influences on these disputes: roles of "great" powers and of other nations.
IV. What is the significance of the disputed areas to the parties?
V. Summary of solutions and possible actions.

During the first meeting of the Assembly, participants failed to engage the substantive issues outlined. Process issues once again prevented substantive discussion. Disagreement centered on the formality of the Assembly meetings, with the chairman asserting strict parliamentary procedure and a few members challenging his authority. A related implicit issue was how to handle the deviant and obstructionist behavior exhibited by one member whose disruptions prevented any constructive dialogue. The Assembly ended with a decision to resume discussion on Friday morning in Working Groups I and II. In one sense the participants were retreating to their more familiar workgroups.

Weekend Break

The two-day break from Friday noon to Sunday noon allowed for some diversion. After an organized bus trip to Venice, which most of the participants took, all were able to return to the activity with renewed vigor.

However, a bit of disconcerting news had reached members of the workshop. Tribal tensions in Kenya had increased during the previous month with the assassination of Tom Mboya, a leader of the Luo tribe. Mboya had been considered a possible successor to Jomo Kenyatta, a Kikuyu and present head of the government. The Kenyan group included members of both tribes. The *London Times* reported developments in the apprehending of a Kikuyu charged with slaying Mboya, and also reported charges of tribal oath-taking by Kikuyu. Two Kenyans were especially upset by the continuing unrest that this chain of events promised for their country.

Resuming Dialogue in the Groups

Sunday afternoon Group II resumed the discussion it had stopped Friday noon. In addition, the issue of ethnic prejudice was acknowledged and treated briefly. The discussion revealed significant diversity within the three national groups in terms of conciliatory versus adamant views on the conflict issues.

Brainstorming

Later that evening, the consultants introduced the technique of brainstorming and practiced it on solutions to a war occurring elsewhere in Africa so that it could be employed if and when it was deemed useful to problem solving of their own border disputes.

The committee then convened the Assembly to proceed with the substantive discussions of the dispute. Most participants felt the need to engage issues in the total community. However, when the Assembly convened, a serious tone could not be maintained; nervous joking was only heightened by the chairman's strict adherence to parliamentary procedure. After a few unsuccessful efforts to initiate a serious discussion, a move to adjourn carried. Participants and staff were unhappy about their ineffectiveness in this Assembly.

Ideation in the Group

Monday's sessions were marked by a cooperative effort to develop ideas for a solution of the border problems. Working Group II decided to break up into two subgroups and brainstorm. They generated 150 ideas, categorizing them into political and economic, military, and social solutions, and assigned them to three subgroups for further development.

By that evening two subgroups were progressing well, but the third had hit a snag when dealing with the problem of development and administration of the disputed areas. This group had explored methods for implementing one political strategy, namely, "freezing the question of sovereignty for ten years," during which "free movement" would be guaranteed. The snag developed over what territories should be included in the free movement zone. Several possibilities had been debated.

When this third subgroup reported, S_5 became adamant on the Somali position. Several emotional interchanges ensued between S_5 and two Ethiopians. Because the stance taken by S_5 seemed to admit of no solution other than the one he preferred, one consultant urged S_5 to ask himself whether political compromise might not be required in any conceivable outcome. In what seemed to be an effort to offer some hope, S_5 replied that he could visualize compromises but ones that took other forms. The discussion ended on that note.

Participants generally expressed the feeling that the day had been the most productive thus far. They also preferred to continue in the small groups within Group II and to meet in the Assembly only when the group had worked through to some operational delineation of the basic controversial issues.

The Yale and consulting staffs met later that evening after a long and exhausting day. Group I's day had been less productive, and the staff from that group was depressed; although it had used many of the same procedures for working the problem, dissident members had frustrated the work.

Merging the Two Group Proposals in the Planning Committee

The planning committee met Tuesday evening to integrate the two groups' proposals. Group II's proposal was elaborate and typewritten. Group I's proposal was more sketchy. The committee tried to resolve as many differences between the documents as possible; but when this failed, it stated the alternatives for floor debate in the Assembly on Wednesday.

Major differences were identified: (1) Should there be recognition of ultimate right of self-determination and provision for a plebiscite? Group II included this proposal; Group I clearly avoided such recognition and provision. (2) Should the neutral or buffer zone be wholly from within the disputed territory, as Group II recommended, or include territory clearly now within the Somali Republic, as recommended by Group I? These differences were treated as "alternatives" within an otherwise consolidated document — largely the language, format, and content of Group II's proposal.

To compare the two documents, Group I's proposals were relatively closer to the general views of the governments of Kenya and Ethiopia; and Group II's were relatively closer to those of the Somali Republic. We learned that a few of the Somalis in Group II had voiced disappointment with one or more of their brethren in Group I, and that a few Kenyans and a few Ethiopians in Group I disapproved of the positions taken by their fellow countrymen in Group II. National groups caucused that evening. There were no grounds for optimism that the workshop participants would reach unanimous agreement on a specific proposal. On the other hand, each of the two working groups, with its multicountry membership, had been able to generate a proposal generally supported by its membership.

Deterioration of the Process in the Assembly

A Kenyan, K_4, chaired the Assembly on Wednesday. He had emerged as a gifted, articulate, and serious participant and his views on the border disputes were intermediate in terms of the spectrum created by the workshop participants. Very early in this session, one Somali sensed the likely direction of the day's development and was prompted to give the warning contained in a Somali proverb, "One must not follow his footprints back." He was correct in sensing that in some respects we were to retrace our steps of the past few days. The following illustrate the tone:

E_1 (in disgust): I object to this merged document.

E_1 went on to express disapproval: first, that the documents had been merged; second, that Group I's proposals were incorporated into Group II's format rather than vice versa; third, that the Committee failed to incorporate all of Group I's ideas into the merged document. Finally, he disagreed with the content of most of the proposals in the document.

O_2: The two conflict issues are self-determination and the scope of the region.

K_1: The mere reference to the right of self-determination will signal an intention ultimately to cede the disputed area to the Somali Republic. This is completely unacceptable.

K_4: The spirit was to reduce direct confrontation between our states. Therefore, we ought to stick to the idea of a buffer zone.

S_5: Let's state self-determination as a right of the peoples involved. We should not use the criteria of what is acceptable to the governments.

E_1: I speak both as an individual and an Ethiopian. The particular regime is not important. I am going to have to live with any position I take here. The fact that I am an Ethiopian is a reality for me.

Some differences of opinion were then expressed by persons from the same country. For example, E_6 differentiated his view from that just expressed by E_1.

E_1 (turning to confront S_1): By what right, by what idea of justice do you ask us to give up people and territory to the Somali Republic?

S_1: We are talking about self-determination, not annexation.

K_1: In this situation, they are the same!

•

•

•

K_1: I am growing very angry. Somalia is like a woman who is asking for something, but with nothing to give.

C_2: Our two groups were microcosms of this larger Assembly. We were able to reach agreement in them. Why can't we here?

K_4: There are areas of agreement on which we can build: (1) We all want a solution. (2) We agree on some buffer zones. (3) We all want unity eventually. The areas of disagreement are the right of self-determination and its exercise.

S_1: The man who dies in the first clash of the fighting is deaf to reason. This is not meant as a threat to K_1. We should — in our emotional state — turn to a positive proposal of federation, lifting boundaries. Our problems are with our own governments.

There followed a futile attempt to rebuild some sense of common purpose among participants, based on the idea of larger schemes of cooperation. Unfortunately, when the Assembly reconvened in the afternoon, there was no change in sentiment or patterns of participation. The following are excerpts from the Wednesday afternoon meeting.

E_1: It is not becoming to a sovereign state to abrogate its rights of administration in its own territory. I accept only a small buffer zone that is free of armies, but that is all.

S_4: The arms are a consequence of the real problem. The real problem is one of sovereignty. Dealing with arms won't solve the problem.

S_2: Unless there is recognition of the underlying problems involving land, life patterns, territorial claims, we are wasting our time.

E_2 (taking a more conciliatory stand than E_1): I'd go a step further than a buffer zone and have us pour resources into the development of the neutralized zone.

S_5 (continuing the debate tone): That would acknowledge that there is a sovereignty issue!

E_3 (trying to recapture the incentives for searching for an accommodation): Let us focus on the costs of continuing the dispute.

K_1: I agree with E_1. As a Kenyan nationalist, I state we are not prepared to compromise our boundaries. We are not prepared to compromise on our nationals. I do accept a buffer zone as an experiment in cooperation, but . . . I've been called a warrior by my group. Maybe the Somalis are suffering from ethnocentrism.

•

•

•

E_1: I'm beginning to be suspicious of the underlying sinister motives of my Somali brothers.

At this point C_3 observed that they had reached an apparent impasse in the discussions but also noted that not everyone had been involved in the discussion. (The antagonism and debate had involved exchanges primarily among members of Group I.) C_3 raised the question of whether some regrouping or some other approach to the subject might not allow for movement. He made no formal recommendation for regrouping but moved that the Assembly break and allow the planning committee to consider ways of getting by the impasse.

After some debate, the Assembly decided to take a break. Members of the committee agreed that the discussion had turned to reiteration of extreme nationalistic views and had become less and less compromise oriented. The planning committee decided to suggest that the Assembly focus on short-run solutions and avoid the issue of self-determination, which most members agreed had stimulated much of the suspicion.

When the Assembly reconvened, and after K_4 presented the idea of focusing on short-run solutions, K_1 reiterated his adamant no-compromise stand. S_2, E_2, S_1, and E_4 tried to initiate some positive note but failed. Hostility increased still further when E_1 asserted that the planning committee was not neutral because in combining the proposals it had omitted two possible outcomes from the plebiscite: namely, voting to remain with Ethiopia or Kenya and neutralization. E_3 tried to reassure him that it was an oversight.

The meeting ended on a confused note. Many were reluctant to agree to return to the Assembly to continue work. The Assembly adjourned on a note of general pessimism.

The Assembly met after dinner but soon adjourned the substantive meeting. In urging adjournment one Somali reminded others that he had been called a cheater earlier in the day and he did not want to suffer any further such statements. "Besides," he said, "Somalis are warriors and I am likely to become violent." (Earlier in the day, his facial expression had revealed extreme distress, although he was not participating verbally in the discussion.) A second Somali feared that continued discussion could only damage the many friendships that had developed over the two weeks.

One of the organizers made a brief speech to the effect that it had been a high-risk, high-payoff enterprise and that the eventual outcome was still in question. He went on to say, "Maybe the conference will have sparked an idea that leads to some resolution of the dispute. Maybe methodologically this approach will be better understood and therefore applied in other international situations. One simply cannot evaluate the workshop at this point in time. In any event, we cannot afford not to keep trying." He expressed thanks to everyone participating.

The final morning, participants left Hotel Fermeda in various groupings, with plans to go back to their respective African nations either directly or indirectly.

Outcomes

The Fermeda workshop ended on a sour note. The developments late in the meeting resulted in part from very knotty issues at the heart of the border disputes and in part from features of the design of this particular workshop.

The ultimate purpose was to have some positive influence on the resolution of the border disputes between Somalia and both Kenya and Ethiopia. The workshop participants were debriefed by their governments. Also, during the month following the workshop a meeting took place in Addis Ababa between the prime minister of Somalia and the emperor of Ethiopia. However, armed battles were to recur between Somalia and Ethiopia over the next decade.

What about the more limited aims of the workshop? On the one hand, there were clear failures in terms of two of the staff's criteria for measuring immediate effectiveness. First, the workshop was unable to reach a consensus about a proposed solution. Second, the workshop community did not transfer to the Assembly the trust, confidence, and problem-solving process it had developed earlier in the groups. These assessments are discussed below in connection with the design decisions that affected them.

On the other hand, the workshop had succeeded in creating productive processes and positive results in the two working groups. There were further positive by-products reported by participants. The planning committee had approved the development and use of a questionnaire to help evaluate aspects of this experiment. The questionnaire was administered when the mood of members was basically depressed, on the last evening of the Assembly, and it was to be returned completed, but unsigned, to a staff member's mailbox later that evening or the next morning. Fourteen of eighteen participants returned their questionnaires. Since not returning a questionnaire might have been an expression of negative feelings toward the workshop, a conservative interpretation of the results is appropriate.

The questionnaire results confirmed that participants found the cross-cultural discussions educational; that they had achieved better understanding of one another's views; that they had gained some insight into their own communication skills and other aspects of group process; and that they believed members of the workshop had developed moderately more open attitudes toward possible solutions of the disputes. These participants' responses tended to confirm what the staff had assumed: namely, that while the polarization of nationalistic views, the dissolution of earlier areas of agreement, and the expressions of hostility and suspicion characterized the behavior in the Assembly, they did not represent a generalized pattern of movement in the attitudes of the majority of individuals.

Participants also were asked: "To what extent do you believe the workshop has produced innovative ideas relevant to solving the problems between Ethiopia and Somalia and between Kenya and Somalia?" Most respondents reported "small extent."

Implications for Dialogue in Intergroup Settings

What can we learn from the Fermeda workshop about the general challenge of promoting dialogue in intergroup settings? Do the concepts and methods of the dialogue approach described in Chapters 6, 7, and 8 apply? What modifications and additions are required?

The interpersonal dialogues in both the organizational contexts and the intergroup setting illustrated by the Fermeda workshop were attempts to develop improved relationships between participants and other capacities of the participants to integrate or balance their interests.

There are, however, basic structural differences between the interpersonal dialogues in organizational contexts and those in the Fermeda workshop, which had major implications for the management of dialogue: The Fermeda participants worked on relationships, but they were not ongoing relationships. The Fermeda parties comprised a number of participants, not an individual. And, as pointed out earlier, the Fermeda objective was to generate a promising solution but not to act on it.

Other types of intergroup settings which may be of more direct relevance to the readers combine the features of both of the dialogue settings illustrated in this book. Consider union–management relations, where the urgent need for better management of differences is widely recognized. Heightened competitive threat has produced an imperative in many unionized industries for unions and managements to enter into new forms of partnership. In Eastern Air Lines, the pilots', machinists', and attendants' unions are all represented on the board of directors and a role for employees and their representative in key management decisions is ensured by other mechanisms. In General Motors, management and the United Auto Workers have entered into collaborative institutional arrangements in certain plants, such as the Fiero plant, and certain projects, such as the Saturn, which would have been unthinkable a decade ago. These are but the more dramatic examples of a general trend. And their future success is uncertain. The point is that these new structures and institutional roles will be no better than the relationships that exist between the institutions and their respective leaders.

Transformation of the labor–management relationship usually involves, at the minimum, direct meetings between key leaders on both sides. Whether the meetings are one-on-one or two-on-two and whether they take place with or without a third party, the two leaders explore the past and current costs and causes of distrust, including their own contributions to the pattern. There invariably are other meetings to undertake similar work involving teams from both sides, often a meeting lasting a couple of days in a relaxing environment. In some cases most of the direct efforts to change the working relationship between the key leaders occurs during these off-site workshops. Thus, these efforts have many of the characteristics of the type of interpersonal dialogue that occurs within organizational settings, and some of the additional characteristics illustrated by the Fermeda workshop.

We now turn to a review of the Fermeda dialogue in terms of the ideas presented in Chapters 6–8 about strategic ingredients, techniques, and third-party roles, deriving the more general implications for interpersonal dialogue in intergroup settings.

Strategic Functions Promoting Dialogue

Are the seven strategic ingredients outlined in Chapter 6 applicable to the intergroup setting? I conclude that they are all broadly relevant, although, as the Fermeda case illustrates, these requirements take different and often more complex forms. Also, for intergroup dialogue there is an additional requirement, intragroup coherence.

1. Intragroup Coherence

We address this requirement first because it arises out of the major structural differences between one-on-one dialogues and the group-to-group dialogues typical of intergroup workshops. Moreover, the presence of multiple representatives of an interest group complicates the provision of the other seven conditions.

Internal differences often are a reality for both (or all) of the back home groups represented in the workshop but if these intragroup differences are significant and are not managed during the workshop, the intergroup dialogue cannot be productive. At Fermeda better relations within national groups could have improved the quality of the deliberations during the last two days and the likelihood that the community would converge on some areas of substantive agreement. We explore later several third-party techniques and tactics which relate to intragroup cohesion.

2. Motivation

The Yale organizers worked for three years to get a green light simultaneously from all three countries; and they worked carefully to recruit eighteen appropriate individuals who were sufficiently interested to invest their time and energy in the effort. The motivation that resulted was not entirely symmetrical. Somalia's representatives generally were more vitally concerned. For example, the parents of one of the Somali participants were nomads in the Ogaden at the time we met. Moreover, the strength of interest in generating solutions varied among those from the same country. These intergroup differences affected the productivity of the dialogue.

3. Situational Power

On the face of it, there was a lack of symmetry in power in the situation because both Kenya and Ethiopia had significant border disputes with the smaller Somalia but not with each other. This was somewhat offset by two factors favoring the Somalis: they had the higher intensity of interest in the disputes, and the workshop method of conflict resolution by dialogue between peers was a more natural one in the Somali culture than in the other African cultures represented. Ethiopians in particular were oriented to having a superior hear the merits of contending parties and render an impartial judgment. All factors considered, the situational power was adequately balanced for the work that needed to be done.

It should be noted that the closeness of Ethiopia to the United States and Kenya to Great Britain could have been an allying force on the Kenya and Ethiopian participants, considering the closeness of Somalia to the Soviet Union; however, this did not appear to be a factor operating in this particular situation.

4. *Synchronizing*

The importance of this requirement in the Fermeda workshop is illustrated by an instance of omission. A major step in the transition from work on developing relationships to putting them to work on the issues was a procedure for exchanging perceptions of the other group and self-perceptions. When the Somalis did but the others did not follow the prescribed format for this exchange, the Somalis were angry and become more cautious. We return to this incident later in our discussion of techniques.

5. *Pacing*

Managing the differentiation and integrative phases was important in Fermeda. However, because the participants did not have any histories of personal conflict with each other, one task was to prevent the generalized intergroup conflict from getting personalized in these relationships. The consultants provided integrative experiences early in the workshop, knowing that differences would need to be addressed as they happened. They deliberately held off discussion of the more divisive substantive issue while working relationships were being developed. Thus, pacing integrative and differentiation activities was as important to Fermeda as to our organizational conflicts, but the absence of an ongoing relationship called for a different sequencing strategy.

6. *Openness*

This ingredient was extremely important in Fermeda, an importance underscored by direct evidence of the crippling inhibitions that developed late in the workshop — as the issues became stickier and as the prospect of returning home became more salient. In addition to the factors that operate in an organizational context, the absence of intragroup harmony has a major influence on openness in an intergroup setting such as Fermeda.

7. *Communications*

This important requirement may often be difficult to achieve in an intergroup setting, but there did not happen to be any special aspects to this requirement in the Fermeda setting, due in part to the participants' common background of education in British or American universities.

8. *Tension Level*

Maintaining a productive level of tension was a major challenge in Fermeda, as it would be in other intergroup settings where feelings of individuals are strong and are also shared by their fellow group members. Thus, an individual's feelings and conflictful behavior are not only influenced by provocative remarks by the other side but are reinforced and amplified by one's fellow group members. The Fermeda third party was remarkably successful in this respect while the workshop community was young and most fragile, but it was not able to reduce the tension that mounted in the latter stages.

Techniques and Tactical Choices

In Chapter 7 we analyzed the techniques and actions that served to supply the necessary ingredients and otherwise influenced the productivity of confrontation. Not surprisingly, many of the techniques and tactical issues that figured in the Fermeda workshop were different from those analyzed in the organizational context. We will emphasize these in the discussion below because they are indicative of the tactical issues important to dialogue in intergroup settings generally.

1. *Composition*

Deciding the composition of the intergroup workshop presents many more issues of choice than were involved in the organizational dialogues. And these choices may have significant influence on the effectiveness of the dialogue, as they did in the Fermeda case. Five aspects of the composition of the Fermeda workshop illustrate its importance.

First, the intellectual and emotional attributes of participants influence the effectiveness of dialogue. The majority of the six participants from each African country were bright, articulate, and emotionally mature. This, together with their diverse backgrounds, produced an extraordinarily high quality of discussion. The format encouraged openness about feelings as well as thought, but some persons were more comfortable than others with the expression of affect — love, hate, rejection, anger, regret, shame, guilt, hope, despair, compassion, or disappointment. Those who tended to suppress or deny such feelings were less able to engage in authentic communication and to build interpersonal trust quickly. The effect of some inhibited participants was to slow down the development of trusting relationships. Also, the presence of even one person who lacks emotional maturity and who has abnormally high self-oriented needs — for example, for attention or to be counterdependent — can seriously distort, even completely disrupt, a workshop. In Fermeda the self-oriented needs of at least one member had such an effect.

Second, the participants' information and interest in the specific intergroup issues must be considered. Two Fermeda participants did not evidence a sufficiently high interest in the dispute to make the emotional and intellectual investment the workshop required. Other participants, whose normal roles in society did not necessarily give them much familiarity with the history of the dispute, were uneven in their background knowledge.

A third aspect of the composition is how closely participants are associated with those who can make the decisions that commit their group. In some settings, such as labor and management, the leadership staff may participate. In other cases, this is impossible or undesirable. In the Fermeda case, the basic concept was for the dialogues to occur outside of formal diplomatic channels. It was determined that because problem solving requires an exploratory stance, the participants selected should not be obliged to advance their government's position. But because a raison d'être for the workshop also must be communicated to the respective governments, it was desirable to include persons who have the confidence of their government. Thus, one should seek some optimal level of association with the current governments. In this respect the Fermeda participants were generally appropriate for this first workshop of its kind.

Fourth, the reactions that exist among the members of a group must be considered. One could argue that if the workshop premise is that individuals are acting on the basis of their own views, opinions, and insights rather than representing a government, or some other authority, one need not be concerned about the quality of relations among the participating members of the group. The reply is that in a workshop such as Fermeda the value of the team is not to ensure that its members can develop a common position and a coordinated strategy of influence, a capacity that would be considered desirable in a more traditional diplomatic context. Instead, one wants a group marked by mutual respect and trust such that it can tolerate differences in viewpoints among its members. A person must be able to explore and "try on" a position at variance with his or her government without eliciting social pressure from other representatives of the same country during the workshop. Participants also must feel secure that when they return home they will not be subject to charges that they made unpatriotic statements.

Therefore, the relations among members from a group should be considered in composing the workshop. If antagonism exists among group members at the outset of the workshop, then the integration of individuals into a total workshop community will take more time. If the divisions — whether based on personality, ethnic membership, social class, or ideology — are so basic as to persist throughout the workshop (as they did in some instances at Fermeda), then they will seriously limit the quality and extent of the exploration for innovative solutions.

Although the ideal of high intragroup trust encourages less diversity, other considerations encourage maximum diversity. For example, a group of participants with sufficient diversity can realistically represent and mirror the views of the various forces or factions that exist in the back home group in question. It is also true that in reporting the workshop results a diverse set of participants will have more credibility with the groups it represents. Again the idea is to achieve optimum diversity.

A fifth composition question is whether to include a set of participants who are peers in the group or to include a leader (or create a leadership role). In the Fermeda case, no member of a national group was expected to play any kind of leadership role before, during, or after the workshop. This encouraged individual responses and allowed informal leadership to emerge as appropriate to the workshop setting. However, neither any individual in a national group nor the group as a whole had any formally sanctioned structure for dealing with the problem of a disruptive member. Hence the disruptive member at Fermeda was dealt with either in the working group or individually by one of the Yale organizers.

2. Context

Structuring the context for dialogue was equally important in the intergroup and organizational settings and involved similar considerations. The Fermeda case illustrates the importance of duration, location, and the physical setting.

Two weeks turned out to be inadequate. On the one hand, time is required to learn to function as a group, to develop relations and communications in all of the groupings instrumental to the success of the workshop, to explore the background to the problem, to discuss peripheral and central issues, to be able to disengage from the hard task work and return to it fresh, to "sleep on" apparently acceptable solutions before becoming committed to them, and to disengage from impasses in order to reapproach them later. On the other hand, a sense of urgency can facilitate such activities as getting acquainted, background discussion, exploring issues, generating solutions, and converging on areas of agreement.

The Fermeda workshop was too short for at least four activities: (1) developing national groups, (2) developing the total community into a well-functioning group, (3) "sleeping on" the tentative proposed solutions before they were submitted to the Assembly, and (4) retreating from impasses — for example, over the principle of self-determination — in order to break the individual mental sets and the polarized social dynamics and thereby allow for new approaches. The workshop simply had run out of time when these needs became so pressing and apparent. As a practical matter, it would have been difficult to lengthen substantially the experimental Fermeda workshop.

The adequacy of time depends upon workshop composition. If the workshop community is composed of persons characterized by high intellectual skills, familiarity with the background of the issues, personal openness, and prior positive relations among national group members, then the optimal duration of the workshop is shorter.

Northern Italy was a favorable location. In political terms Italy was neutral territory. It was also sufficiently isolated from family and professional distractions. The paucity of news on Kenya, Ethiopia, and Somalia in the Italian news media reduced, but did not eliminate, the political distractions.

Insulation allows for a deeper immersion in the mental and emotional processes of the workshop and permits the development of a "cultural island," which in turn encourages participants to challenge cherished assumptions, break old thought processes, and modify attitudes. However, because the attitudes, views, and products generated by the workshop must eventually be persuasive also to countrymen who have not attended the workshop, it is possible for the cultural island effect to be too complete if it leads to proposed solutions that will later be dismissed out of hand back home as unrealistic or idealistic. Fermeda probably was close to optimal for this particular workshop. The physical setting was ideal. The lofty and inspiring mountain view at Fermeda together with the sunny but brisk weather reinforced the desired mood, and the mountain paths invited brief walks that complemented the sedentary workshop meetings. Meals were taken at small tables, generally filled as participants arrived, a practice that invariably produced an international mixture.

3. *Process*

Managing one-to-one and group-to-group dialogue requires somewhat different techniques. In the two-person conflict encounters, a third party can influence the content and process of the dialogue by verbal interventions formulated on the spot as the dialogue unfolds. In an intergroup setting, working with a larger and more complex social system, there is utility to considering a variety of structured stimuli and a variety of such groupings. These require more explicit advance planning and coordination.

In Fermeda the third-party group utilized simulations and presented brief conceptual lectures. Although these activities had varied yields, they probably were worth the time. Ideally, they would have been more tailored to the situation. The more effective work at Fermeda occurred in the two working groups. It was in these working groups that the issues of rivalry, membership, and trust were managed; and authentic communication, relationships, and patterns of mutual influence were developed. As the workshop progressed, these groups spent more and more time directly on the border disputes.

The least effective grouping was the national groups. In Rome the consultants had considered but rejected a design in which a consultant would work with each national group before turning to the development of groupings with multinational composition. The design argument that prevailed was based on the principle of primacy: Give early emphasis to interpersonal relationships that cut across country groups because they are expected to be the more difficult to establish. It was feared that by giving reinforcement to national identification early in the workshop, in-group solidarity would be increased and relationships across national groups would be more difficult to attain.

When the workshop finally did provide for work within the three national groups on the fifth day, the participants were reluctant to work in these groups. These avoidance tendencies were based on distrust, especially strong within the Kenyan group and moderately strong among the Ethiopians. The planning committee rejected the consultants' suggestion for more scheduled meetings of national groups along with a consultant assisting each of these groups. Private ad hoc caucuses by nationals did occur on the final two days, but they involved sharp differences and instances of strong influence attempts.

The third grouping, the Assembly, also failed to become effective. On many occasions during the first five days, the total community was assembled for a simulation or presentation, typically followed by open discussion. When focus shifted to the dispute and the task of creating a single document became more salient, the need for total community discussion and decision making became more compelling. The planning committee created the Assembly for this purpose.

The Assembly started on a note of confusion and ended on a note of frustration and anger. The ineffectiveness of the Assembly resulted from several factors: (1) the disruptive actions of one participant, (2) the fact that it was a new group with all of the attendant issues of rivalry and identity conflict in the interpersonal relationships across working groups, (3) the existence of important tensions between nationals who had heretofore been in separate working groups, and (4) the abrupt shift from the fluid structure and spontaneity of the working groups to the constraining framework of parliamentary procedure.

Although the parliamentary procedure was a method for coping with the first three factors — the disruptive person, the "new group" phenomenon, and tensions among nationals — the Assembly relied upon parliamentary procedure for other reasons as well. First, it is a habitual response to treating the institutional affairs of universities and matters of state. Second, as the workshop came closer to making choices about proposed solutions, the stakes became higher; and individuals may have increasingly preferred procedures that were both predictable and impersonal.

One effect of the parliamentary procedure was to seriously circumscribe the effectiveness of the process consultants as long as they abided by the same rules; for example, they, too, had to queue up and seek recognition by the chair before they intervened in the Assembly process. Unfortunately, they did not make an issue of the constraint, for if they had they might well have been legitimately exempted from the rule; since they were not making substantive contributions, special access to make process interventions would not have been considered out of order.

4. The Goal for the Workshop

The formulation of an agreed goal for the dialogue would appear to be more important in the intergroup workshop setting than in the organizational setting. The basic substantive purpose of the Fremeda workshop was to contribute solutions that might strengthen peace and security in the Horn of Africa. That was a given. However, when the staff met in Rome, the operational goal stated by the Yale sponsors was to reach consensus on a single proposal. Setting that goal may have been an error.

The Fermeda workshop was unable to reach consensus on a proposal. Was that goal too ambitious? Again the concept of optimality is necessary. The operational goal for a workshop can be set too low, when it does not really challenge, or too high, when it carries too high a risk of failure.

The Fermeda goal can be questioned on another basis. If achieved, would a single proposal facilitate or hinder the formal negotiations that ultimately would take place between governments? It could hinder them if one government used the workshop's proposal as a point of departure, because the second government might be forced to dissociate itself from the workshop and its product. However, if the workshop's goal had been to develop alternative solutions, each of which received some international support in the workshop, these documents would allow more flexibility for negotiations between governments.

Third-Party Roles

The same role attributes that we identified in Chapter 8 as helpful to third-party facilitators in organizational settings apply to intergroup settings. In Fermeda, the third parties appeared to be acceptable to the participants. Initially some participants speculated that the staff might be connected with the U.S. Central Intelligence Agency. Presumably this particular concern declined over the course of the workshop. The fact that the organizers were white citizens of a country associated with colonialism did not prove to be the drawback we anticipated. Supporting evidence for this conclusion is provided by participants' responses to the following questionnaire item:

> In your opinion, to what extent did the fact that the organizers and trainers were Americans rather than Africans constitute an advantage or disadvantage?

Of the thirteen responses to this question, only one indicated that it was "some net disadvantage." Six participants checked the phrase "as much advantage as disadvantage," three participants said it was "some net advantage," and three indicated it was "very much an advantage." Overall, the African participants had invested their confidence in the Yale professors and then were willing to transfer this confidence to the consultants.

However, one particular attribute assumes different importance in the intergroup setting, namely control over process. This is illustrated by the Fermeda workshop. At the outset the third-party organizers and consultants could determine groupings and agenda, as well as intervene into the ongoing dialogue. As the community developed, including the increasing sense of ownership of participants over the workshop process and its outcomes, the third-party group had to share power, finally by yielding effective decision making over process to a representative steering committee. As appropriate as this was, it meant that in the end, the third-party consultants were less able to intervene in ways to promote dialogue. This issue is less likely to arise in one-on-one dialogues where the third party's interventions are mostly verbal and can be quickly ignored or accepted on their merits.

Summary

The chapter describes and analyzes a dialogue workshop on the border disputes in the Horn of Africa. The structure for the situation differed from the interpersonal dialogues analyzed in earlier chapters in that the participants did not have prior relationships, could generate new solutions but could not implement them, and came in groups. These differences helped account for some of the unique challenges represented by this workshop. Dialogue in other settings, such as labor and management, often have some characteristics similar to our organizational ones and other characteristics similiar to those in the international workshop example.

I conclude that the approach to interpersonal dialogue and third-party facilitation that was first formulated in organizational contexts is generally applicable to intergroup settings. However, there is at least one adaptation that must be made to the basic concept: if the intergroup setting involves group-on-group exchanges, an additional strategic function becomes crucial, namely, ensuring an adequate level of internal coherence within each group. Moreover, there also are certain techniques and tactical choices that are unique or assume a different importance when the dialogue concept is extended to the intergroup setting; in particular those involving the composition of the workshop groups, the groupings and subgroupings for work during the workshop, and the operational goals for the workshop.

References

Burton, J. W. *Conflict and Communication: The Use of Controlled Communication in International Relations.* London: Macmillan, 1969.

Doob, L. W. "The Belfast Workshop: An Application of Group Techniques to a Destructive Conflict." *Journal of Conflict Resolution* 17, no. 3 (1973):489–512.

Doob, L. W., ed. *Resolving Conflict in Africa: The Fermeda Workshop.* New Haven: Yale University Press, 1970.

Doob, L. W., ed. "A Cyprus Workshop: Intervention Methodology during a Continuing Crisis." *Journal of Social Psychology* 98 (1976): 143–44.

Hill, B. J. "An Analysis of Conflict Resolution Techniques: From Problem-Solving Workshops to Theory." *Journal of Conflict Resolution* 26 (1982):109–138.

Kelman, H. C. "An Interactional Approach to Conflict Resolution and Its Application to Israeli–Palestinian Relations." *International Interactions* 6, no. 2 (1979):99–122.

Walton, R. E. "A Problem-Solving Workshop on Border Conflicts in Eastern Africa." *Journal of Applied Behavioral Science* 6, no. 4 (1970):453–89.

10

Summary and Conclusions

This book is intended to contribute to both the theory and practice of the management of conflict, both intraorganizational and intergroup conflict. The three cases taken from organizational contexts provided an empirical basis for constructing a middle-range theory of interpersonal dialogue and third-party consultation. The chain of reasoning employed in developing the subject matter runs along the following lines. First, I identified several aspects of a conflict cycle that make conflict subject to controls — controls that may be utilized with or without the parties' directly confronting each other, but which will be more effective if developed jointly by the parties through dialogue. Second, because there are potential risks as well as gains that accompany the use of direct dialogue, I hypothesized strategic factors that enhance the likelihood of successful dialogues. Third, those strategic requirements give meaning to the subsequent treatment of the tactical management of dialogue, whether enacted by participants themselves or by third parties. The inference process was extended to determining the attributes that facilitate the work of the third party.

Once the basic theory was explained, the dialogue concept was applied to an intergroup setting. The basic concept and method were applicable, but additional dimensions to the intergroup setting required attention to another major ingredient for success and to a number of additional tactical issues. In both organizational and intergroup settings our focus was on managing the interpersonal dialogues and our interest was in improving the quality of the working relationship and its problem-solving capacity.

Aspects of Interpersonal Conflict and Their Implications

The diagnostic model of conflict episodes involves four basic elements — issues, triggering events, conflict or conflict-resolving acts of the principals, and their consequences. Interpersonal conflicts are cyclical, following cycles of manifestation and latency, and they are dynamic, changing from one cycle to the next.

Escalation results from the tendency for issues to proliferate: disputants may introduce new issues for tactical reasons or cope with the consequences of conflict in a way that exacerbates, rather than minimizes, the conflict. Escalation also results when conflict resolution moves are not reciprocated. One objective of conflict management is to interrupt self-maintaining and escalating cycles and initiate de-escalating cycles of behavior. Each of several elements of a conflict episode offers a "handle" for controlling conflict.

If one understands the types of events that are capable of triggering a new conflict cycle in a particular interpersonal relationship, one may be able to choose the right time and place for the conflict to occur, and temporarily or permanently to control the conflict and its costs.

If one can impose constraints on the way a conflict manifests itself (for example, by outlawing especially destructive or provocative tactics), one may be able to protect the social system from the more disruptive consequences of the conflict and eliminate the sources of escalation, maybe even achieve some de-escalation.

If one or both principals can develop better methods for

coping with the affective consequences of interpersonal conflict, they can function better individually and as a pair even without resolving the issues in dispute. Coping techniques include ventilating one's feelings to friends and obtaining support from them, as well as enlarging one's general tolerance for conflict.

These several control strategies have limitations and involve additional risks. Control strategies that operate by completely avoiding or significantly constraining the form of the manifest conflict may drive the conflict underground, where it becomes less direct but more destructive and more difficult to manage; or they may result in an accumulation of unexpressed feelings that will make the manifest conflict, when it does occur, more intense. A further difficulty lies in preventing manifest conflict by raising the barriers to expression of conflict: such barriers tend to prevent potentially constructive confrontations as well as other tactical interchanges.

Dialogue and Strategic Ingredients

One can handle a conflict merely by allowing the participants to pursue their own respective strategies of avoidance, constraint, and coping. Dialogue not only increases the parties' abilities to develop better control techniques but also offers the possibility for some resolution of the underlying issues.

The productivity of the dialogue hinges upon many factors that either the principals themselves or the third party can influence. The following, stated here as targets of third-party action, are strategic.

1. The third party can assess whether the motivation to reduce the conflict is mutual. If not, dialogue can be avoided or delayed. If both sides are interested, but one has much higher motivation, then the one with the greater motivation can be encouraged to moderate the level of energy invested in the process, the pacing of the dialogue, and expectations about outcomes accordingly.

2. An imbalance in situational power will affect the course of the dialogue, by undermining trust and inhibiting the participants. The third party can attempt to achieve more balance; for

example, offsetting an organizational power advantage of one by involving more allies for the other. The third party can regulate interactions to favor a person with lesser verbal or fighting skills.

3. The third party can ensure that the initiative by one is synchronized with the other's readiness. Otherwise, one risks rejection and misinterpretation; for example, a conciliatory gesture may be interpreted as a sign of weakness, or the expression of negative affect by one may be seen by the other as an attempt to perpetuate the conflict rather than as a gesture of trust and an effort to "get it off my chest."

4. A related function is to ensure either that the differentiation phase of the dialogue is worked out fully before moving on to the integrative phase, or at least, that sufficient differentiation has occurred to provide a basis for the integration contemplated for the time being. The underlying principle is that, given a conflictful history, the potential for genuine integration at any point in time during the confrontation is no greater than the adequacy of the differentiation already achieved. In an intergroup dialogue where there are no personal histories, the phasing task is different. An early emphasis on integrative activity may be designed to avoid creating repeated conflict and to promote a capacity to handle the divisive issues that have not yet been placed on the table.

5. The third party can assess and influence the factors that contribute to openness, norms about the expression of differences, emotional reassurance for participants, and facilitation skills.

6. The third party can increase the reliability of communications: by translating messages; by procedural devices that require the parties in the dialogue to demonstrate that they each understand what the others have said; and by contributing to the development of a common language.

7. The third party can attempt to achieve an optimum level of tension, sometimes raising it in order to create a sense of urgency, and at other times reducing it if it is creating distortion in the communication processes.

8. In intergroup settings the third party can also assess and attempt to influence the internal coherence in each of the disputing groups.

None of these eight ingredients is sufficient and all are necessary in some significant measure for a successful dialogue.

Dialogue Techniques

If the preceding discussion provides a theory of third-party functions, the discussion of tactics below describes the practice of third-party interventions. The two discussions necessarily overlap because one cannot analyze a function without illustrating the behaviors that perform the function. Similarly, one cannot merely list tactical behaviors without some reference to their usefulness. Nevertheless, both functions and tactics need to have their turn at being in the foreground of an analysis of the third-party role.

1. The most passive third-party intervention is to be present in the confrontation. Depending, of course, on the third party's particular personal and role attributes, the mere presence of a third party can perform a synchronization function, influence the group norms governing openness, reassure the participants who see him or her as a source of nonevaluative acceptance, and decrease the perceived risks of failure.

2. One of the active interventions of third parties is their preliminary interviews of the principals, which are used to assess motivation, obtain other relevant information, promote principals' familiarity and experience with the processes of openness and confrontation, establish appropriate third-party role relationships, and provide all concerned with a better basis for deciding whether to proceed toward dialogue.

3. The third party can influence the physical and social context for the dialogue. By choosing a neutral site, one can preserve symmetry in the situational power of participants. By choosing the degree of formality of the setting, one can influence the amount of emphasis on task disagreements versus emotional antagonisms. By arranging for a relatively open-ended time period, one can increase the likelihood that the moves of the principals will be reciprocated in the same session and that some natural pacing of differentiation and integration activities will develop. By determining the composition of the dialogue meeting, the third party can influence the information, support, and perceived risk in the situation. This is especially important in the group-to-group workshop settings.

4. The third party can intervene in the ongoing dialogue process. Each of the following tactical interventions may perform

one of the strategic functions listed above: the third party may initiate agenda, terminate a repetitive discussion, provide equal air time for participants, and reward constructive and punish destructive behavior. The third party may clarify the participants' views by restating, summarizing, and translating each party's views (both explicit and implicit meanings). He or she may encourage the exchange of perceptions and immediate reactions and may give and receive feedback. The third party may provide a diagnosis or encourage a collaborative effort to develop diagnostic insights. The third party may diagnose conditions causing poor dialogue and prescribe discussion techniques that assist the parties in joining issues. He may diagnose conditions causing poor dialogue. The third party may counsel the participants (on coping techniques, for example). In workshop settings the consultant may devise a variety of groupings, each designed to promote different types of work instrumental to the dialogue. He or she may help the parties formulate an operational goal for the workshop dialogue that is both realistic and significant.

5. The third party can assist the principals to prepare for further dialogue. By teaching them what ingredients make a dialogue productive and by identifying for them, in operational form, the techniques and principles that were used effectively in their own immediate experience, the third party can increase the ability of the principals to continue the dialogue on their own. By building other facilitators into the process, the third party can provide for continuing facilitation, if desirable.

Third-Party Attributes

We conclude that certain role attributes are generally optimum for third-party work as described in this book:

1. High professional expertise in social processes is relevant because of the types of diagnosis, behavioral interventions, and emotional support and reassurance required of the third party. In the attempt to be specific and systematic about role behavior, I do not wish to neglect the subtlety of the phenomenon. That is, although I have focused on the general characteristics of the third parties and their overt behaviors, this does not in any way

diminish the clinical skill and interpersonal intuition upon which their behavior is based, and the ingenuity with which their tactical interventions must be conceived if they are to mesh with, yet also influence, the stream of behavior.

2. Low power over the fate of the principals is better because such power tends to inhibit candid interchanges and induce approval-seeking behavior by participants.

3. High control over process is an asset because it allows the third party to take advantage of the tactical opportunities presented by such factors as physical setting, time boundaries, pacing, composition of group, and agenda.

4. At least moderate knowledge about the principals, issues, and background is usually an advantage because it enhances the third party's credibility with the principals and increases the likelihood that the interventions will be on target.

5. Basic third-party neutrality with respect to the substantive issues, the personal relationships with the principals, and the conflict-resolution methodology facilitates the development of principals' trust toward the third-party consultant.

Although the cases and analysis in the book focus on the interventions of third parties who were formally consultants, the implications of the study are broader. Other persons, especially for types of organizational conflict presented here, can perform many of the necessary functions. In the case of dialogue in intergroup settings, neutral third parties formally agreed to by the principals is usually the best route.